Tough Questions:
Christian Answers

ALDERSGATE

Gene Van Note

Editor

Mabeth Clem

Editorial Assistant

Cover Photo: Richard Parker

Photos: 7—Jan Anderson; 25—Anderson; 49—Ace Williams; 61—David Strickler; 100—Wallowitch.

Tough Questions: Christian Answers

Published for the ALDERSGATE ASSOCIATES
By Beacon Hill Press of Kansas City
Kansas City, Missouri

If you looked behind this book—

What would you find?

Your search would uncover a simple statement of purpose. "This book is designed to answer the questions young adults are asking."

"But," you wonder, "how can we be sure that these are the questions of greatest concern to young adults?"

That is a valid query, one that kept intruding into our preliminary planning sessions. So, we interrupted the development of this Dialog book and sent out questionnaires to key churches across North America. Their replies reflect the opinions of more than 1,000 young adults.

On the basis of those returns, we are confident that these are the questions young adults are asking.

Admittedly, they are *tough questions*.

Fortunately, they all have *Christian answers*. That is our quest.

Gene Van Note
Editor

Contents

Chapter 1   What is God like?   6

Chapter 2   Why is there evil in the world?   12

Chapter 3   Why do good people suffer?   23

Chapter 4   Why is life not fair?   28

Chapter 5   Why is there strife and war?   37

Chapter 6   How can we reconcile a God of love
            with a belief in hell?   48

Chapter 7   Are there any grounds for hope?   55

Chapter 8   What is the purpose of life?   61

Chapter 9   How can I know God's will?   67

Chapter 10 Does God answer prayer?   75

Chapter 11 How does man experience God?   85

Chapter 12 Is there a spirit world?   91

Chapter 13 Is there life after death?   99

Chapter 1

Getting to Know God

by Bill Bright

*Background Scriptures: Psalms 90:2; 139:1-4,
6-10; 145:1-7; Revelation 1:8*

Would you like to live a joyful, abundant, and fruitful life—
every day filled with adventure? You can.

You start by getting to know God—who He is and what He
is like—because your concept of God influences every area of
your life: it determines how you relate to yourself, other people,
and every circumstance you encounter.

Do you feel shy, unworthy? A right view of God will change
your attitude toward yourself. Do you hold grudges and resent
other people? Recognizing God's love and forgiveness toward
you will cause you to love and forgive others. Are you con-
fronted with problems that seem insurmountable? A person with
a proper perspective of God's majesty and magnificence can
face difficulties with a thankful and trusting spirit.

In his book *The Knowledge of the Holy,* A. W. Tozer says,

> What comes into our minds when we think about God
> is the most important thing about us. The most portentous
> fact about any man is not what he at a given time may say

or do, but what he in his deep heart conceives God to be like. We tend by a secret law of the soul to move toward our mental image of God.

Were we able to extract from any man a complete answer to the question, "What comes into your mind when you think about God?" we might predict with certainty the spiritual future of that man.

Do you think God is like a divine Santa Claus? A cosmic policeman? A dictator? A big bully?

King David had the right perspective of God. In Psalm 145:1-7 he wrote: "I will praise you, my God and King, and bless your name each day and forever. Great is Jehovah! Greatly praise him! His greatness is beyond discovery! Let each generation tell its children what glorious things he does. I will meditate about

7

your glory, splendor, majesty and miracles. Your awe-inspiring deeds shall be on every tongue; I will proclaim your greatness. Everyone will tell about how good you are, and sing about your righteousness."

David's God was the infinite God of the universe, mighty in power and worthy of this trust. When the armies of Israel were quaking in their boots over the threats of the giant Goliath, the shepherd boy David arrived on the scene and was shocked to discover that one man was causing the entire army of Israel to be afraid.

He asked, "Who is this heathen Philistine, anyway, that he is allowed to defy the armies of the living God?" Then he went forth with five smooth stones and a slingshot to slay Goliath.

One does not meet many heroes of faith like David today. There is a tendency to be superficial in our comprehension of God. There is more busyness than worship in our lives.

Dr. Tozer continues:

The church has surrendered her once lofty concept of God and has substituted for it one so low, so ignoble, as to be utterly unworthy of thinking, worshiping men. With our loss of the sense of majesty has come the further loss of religious awe and consciousness of the divine Presence. We have lost our spirit of worship and our ability to withdraw inwardly to meet God in adoring silence. The words "Be still, and know that I am God" mean next to nothing to the self-confident, bustling worshiper in this middle period of the twentieth century.

A rediscovery of the majesty of God will go a long way toward curing (our troubles). If we would bring back spiritual power to our lives, we must begin to think of God more nearly as He is. The heaviest obligation lying upon the Christian church today is to purify and elevate her concept of God until it is once more worthy of Him—and of her.

I am personally persuaded that if we were to spend more time in the presence of God, worshiping Him, praising Him, adoring Him, reading His Word, and talking with Him in prayer, our faith and witness would be multiplied many times. Let us consider some of the attributes of God—those characteristics that God has disclosed to be true of himself.

8

One of the earliest things that intrigues a child about God is that He is *eternal*. "Where did God come from, Mommy?" he might ask. God has said in His Word, "I am the Alpha and the Omega" (Revelation 1:8)—the beginning and the ending of all things. The Psalmist describes God's eternalness this way: "Before the mountains were created, before the earth was formed, you are God without beginning or end" (Psalm 90:2).

We might better grasp the attribute of eternalness by imagining ourselves as people who are watching the parade of history through a keyhole. All we see are people passing by that keyhole, one or two at a time. But God is, for the sake of this illustration, on a mountain and sees the parade begin and end. With Him there is no such thing as time.

God is also *omnipresent*. He is not limited in space; He is everywhere. Not only is God *with* us, but He also *indwells* us as believers.

I can catch a plane and fly to far-off countries; but no matter where I go, God is with me. There are times of testing, times of temptation, times of adversity, but God is there. He is there in His love to comfort, He is there in His wisdom to give counsel, He is there in His strength to undergird and give support.

Wherever you are or whatever your need, God is there to help you. He is nearer than our hands and feet, closer than our breathing. We can't escape Him. God reminds us in Jeremiah 23:23-24: "Am I a God who is only in one place and cannot see what they are doing? Can anyone hide from Me? Am I not everywhere in all of heaven and earth?"

In Psalm 139:6-10 we read: "This is too glorious, too wonderful to believe! I can never be lost to your spirit! I can never get away from God. If I go up to heaven, you are there; if I go down to the place of the dead, you are there. If I ride the morning winds to the farthest oceans, even there your hand will guide me, your strength will support me."

In his remarkable devotional book, *The Practice of the Presence of God,* Brother Lawrence has much to say to us concerning God's omnipresence. Brother Lawrence was a monk who was assigned to kitchen duty in a monastery. Each task was a chore until he began to realize that everything he did was for the glory of God. He began to practice the presence of God —speaking and acting as if he were in God's very presence. Consequently, that which had been a chore became an adventure—an exciting privilege.

Like Brother Lawrence, we need to have a divine consciousness that God is with us at all times. Only then can we wholeheartedly serve Him in everything we do.

Another attribute of God is His *omniscience.* He knows everything. David says in Psalm 139:1-4, "O Lord, you have examined my heart and know everything about me. You know when I sit or stand. When far away, you know my every thought. You chart the path ahead of me, and tell me where to stop and rest. Every moment, you know where I am. You know what I am going to say before I even say it."

There are occasions when my wife will say, "You read my mind. That was what I was about to tell you." How does that happen? I don't understand it, but I know that if human beings can walk in tune with one another, our capacity is much greater to walk with the Creator of heaven and earth, who is aware of everything concerning us. There is nothing about us that remains unknown to Him; every sin, failure, and weakness is seen and yet He still loves us. What a wonderful God we worship!

The last attribute I want to mention is God's *omnipotence*— His power. He spoke and one hundred billion galaxies were flung into space. Jeremiah talks about God's power in chapter 32, verse 17: "O Lord God! You have made the heavens and earth by your great power; nothing is too hard for you!" And this God loved the world so much that He gave His Son to die on the Cross for our sins.

There is no situation or problem in your life that is too difficult for God to handle. The God whom we worship is the One in whom resides all authority. In His hand is supreme power. If only we believed that our God is all-powerful, we would walk with shoulders erect and head held high. We would have great faith in a great God.

There are other equally important attributes of God—His love, faithfulness, goodness, justice, righteousness, and many others. Study the Word of God for yourself to find out what God is really like, to fall in love with Him and worship Him more than you have ever done in the past. Study, memorize, and meditate on the Word of God, and you will learn to trust Him more. For "faith comes from hearing and hearing by the word of Christ" (Romans 10:17).

I experience great spiritual benefit by thanking and praising God for who He is and what He does—for His love and forgiveness, for His wisdom and power revealed to us through our Lord Jesus Christ. Often I pray through Psalms 139; 145—150; Ephesians 3:20-21; Colossians 3; John 14:12; 15:1-8 and other portions of Scripture, praising and worshiping the Lord for His attributes.

As you meditate upon the greatness of God and His promises, your soul will be bathed with His beauty and holiness. And your understanding of God's character will be reflected in your attitudes and actions throughout the day. Like the Psalmist, you will want to say: "You have let me experience the joys of life and the exquisite pleasures of your own eternal presence" (Psalm 16:11, TLB).

November 1977, *Worldwide Challenge*, as condensed in *The Christian Reader*.

Chapter 2

Where Is God when It Hurts?

by Philip Yancey

Background Scriptures: Romans 8:18-23;
2 Corinthians 4:17-18; 1 Peter 5:10

To the person who suffers, Christianity offers one last contribution, the most important contribution of all. As we have seen, the entire Bible, 3,000 years of history and culture and human drama, focuses like a magnifying glass on the bloody death at Calvary. It is the crux of history, the cornerstone. But it is not the end of the story. Jesus did not stay on the Cross. After three days in a dark tomb, He was seen alive again. Alive! Could it be? His disciples couldn't believe it at first, but He came to them, letting them feel His new body.

Christ brought us the possibility of an afterlife without pain and suffering. All our hurts, then, are temporary. Our future

12

will be painless. Today, we are almost embarrassed to talk about belief in an afterlife complete with rewards and punishments based on our performance on earth. An afterlife seems quaint, cowardly, "a cheap way out" of this world's problems.

(Black Muslims have a funeral custom which rivals some of the Christian funeral customs in its strangeness. When the body is laid out, close friends and family encircle the casket and stand quietly, looking at the dead person. There are no tears, no flowers, no singing. Muslim sisters pass small trays from which everyone takes a thin, round patty of peppermint candy. At a given signal, the onlookers pop the candies in their mouths. Slowly the candies melt, and as they taste the sweetness, they reflect on the sweetness of the life they are commemorating. When the candy is gone . . . that, too, has meaning, for it symbolizes the end of life. It simply dissolves; there is no more.)

Something in man cries out against such a belief. Where do words like *immortal* come from? Why is it murder to kill a man and not a cat?

How can it be noble to agree with the Black Muslims, the materialists, and the Marxists that this world, cancerous with evil and suffering, is the designed end for man? Such a notion only appeared after 7,000 years of recorded history. Every known primitive society and every ancient culture included elaborate beliefs in an afterlife. (Without such beliefs, archaeologists would have a much more difficult task, for the ancients conveniently buried cultural clues in tombs.)

The Coming Change

In contrast, Christians expectantly await a world where every tear will be wiped away and suffering will disappear. We have unusual metaphors to picture the afterlife—streets of gold and gates of pearl, which to the writers symbolized the paragon of luxury. Whatever heaven is, it will banish much of the discomfort of this life and usher in new, unimagined pleasures. We have shadows of it now, fleeting longings that some profound joy, which escapes so quickly here, will one day fill us.

It is as if we are locked in a dark room, as in Sartre's *No Exit*. But chinks of light are seeping through—virtue, glory, hints of truth and justice—convincing us that beyond the walls there exists a world worth all enduring.

The hope which this belief can give to a dying person is starkly illustrated in a 1976 documentary film which was shown on the Public Broadcasting System. Producer-Director Michael Roemer filmed *Dying* in Boston. The film follows the last months' activities of several terminally ill cancer patients. Two, especially, show the extremes of despair and hope.

Harriet and Bill, 33, struggle with a failure of nerve. Nervous about her own future as a widow with two sons, Harriet tells the interviewer: "The sweet girl is being tortured by his cancer. Who's gonna want a widow and 8- and 10-year-old sons? I don't wish him dead, but if he's gotta go, why doesn't he go now?"

In the last weeks of their life together, this family cannot cope with their fears about death. They attack each other, whining and shouting, shattering love and trust. The specter of death is too great.

Rev. Bryant, 56, the dying pastor of a Black Baptist church, provides an amazing contrast. "Right now I'm living some of my greatest moments," he says. "I don't think Rockefeller could be as happy as I am."

The camera crew follows Rev. Bryant as he preaches on death to his congregation, reads the Bible to his grandchildren, and takes a trip South to visit his birthplace. He displays calm serenity and a confidence that he is merely heading home, to a place without pain.

At his funeral, the Baptist choir sings "He's Asleep." And as mourners file past the bier, some reach down to grasp his hand or pat his chest. They are losing a beloved friend, but only for a while. Rev. Bryant is facing a beginning, not an end.

Any discussion of pain is incomplete without this perspective of its temporary nature. A skilled polemist could possibly convince someone that pain is a good thing—better than any of the alternatives God could have allowed. Perhaps. But, actually, pain and suffering are far less than half the picture.

How to imagine eternity? It's so much larger than our short life here that it's hard even to visualize. You can go to a 10-foot chalkboard and draw a line from one side to another. Then, make a one-inch dot in that line. To a microscopic germ cell, sitting in the midst of that one-inch dot, it would look enormous. The cell could spend its lifetime exploring its length and breadth. But you're not a germ cell, you're a human, and by stepping back to view the whole chalkboard you're suddenly struck with how *huge* that 10-foot line is compared to the tiny dot that germ cell calls home.

It's the same way with eternity compared to this life. Seventy years is a long time, and we can develop a lot of ideas about God and how indifferent He appears to suffering in 70 years. But is it reasonable to judge God and His plan for the universe by the swatch of time we spend on earth? No more reasonable than for that germ cell to judge a whole chalkboard by the tiny smudge of chalk where he spends his life. Is that a just trial? Have we missed the perspective of the universe and of timelessness?

Would we complain if God allowed one hour of suffering in an entire lifetime of comfort? He has allowed a lifetime which includes suffering, but that lifetime is a mere hour of eternity.

In the Christian scheme of things, this world and the time spent here are not all there is. Earth is a proving ground, a dot in eternity—but a very important dot, for Jesus said our destiny depends on our obedience here. Next time you want to cry out to God in anguished despair, blaming Him for a miserable world, remember: less than one-millionth of the evidence has been presented, and that one-millionth is being worked out under a rebel flag.

Not Yet

Author Thomas Howard[1] comments that the real pain of suffering is not the present hurt—for martyrs have proved that can be endured. The real pain is that God seems to have His eyes shut, His ears stopped with wax. We read of healings in the Bible, we see others on TV . . . and yet our relatives' bodies, and our own, swell with disease. Where is God? Why is He avoiding us? Why won't He answer?

The response we get is dead silence. Nothing.

The Bible is little help, for along with the healing of the widow of Nain's son are other sons who died. Peter was set loose from prison; John the Baptist was executed. Paul was used to heal people, but his own request for healing was denied.

Howard points to two surprising passages for perspective: the burial of Lazarus and the roadside talk about Jesus' death on the way to Emmaus. Immediately we object, "Yes, but both those stories have happy endings. Too few on earth have such dramatic conclusions." But we can learn from the waiting period in each story: the four days when Lazarus's body rotted in the grave and his family cried tears of disappointment over Jesus' seeming callousness, and the days when the disciples were convinced the entire kingdom had collapsed. Those four days parallel the times of anxious waiting we spend facing pain.

These crushed followers had seen Jesus heal people. Why didn't He act now? Was it that they had too little faith? How, then, to drum up more? In those middle days of gloom, it surely seemed God had deliberately passed them by.

Now, looking back at those stories, we can see how the pieces fit together. In four days, both stories received triumphant endings. Lazarus and Jesus both returned to life. Everyone rejoiced. They actually make better stories because the deaths occurred.

Howard writes of those few days of gloom:

The point is for X-number of days their experience was of defeat. For us, alas, the "X-number of days" may be greatly multiplied. And it is small comfort to us to be told that the difference, then, between us and, say, Mary and Martha's experience of Lazarus' death, or of the two on the road to Emmaus, is only a quantitative difference. "They had to wait four days. You have to wait one, or five, or seventy years. What's the real difference?" That is like telling someone on the rack that his pain is only quantitatively different from mine with my hangnail. The quantity is the difference. But there is, perhaps, at least this much of help for us whose experience is that of Mary and Martha and the others: the experience of the faithful has, in fact, included the experience of utter death. That seems to be

16

part of the pattern, and it would be hard indeed to insist that the death was attributable to some failure of faith on somebody's part.[2]

For all of us, not just Mary and Martha and the two on the road to Emmaus, there will be a personal solution of triumph. There is no slippage with God. He knows when every sparrow falls and has every hair numbered. Every prayer has been heard, even those which might have seemed vacant and useless.

George MacDonald says, "The Lord has come to wipe away our tears. He is doing it; He will have it done as soon as He can; and until He can, He would have them flow without bitterness; to which end He tells us that it is a blessed thing to mourn, because of the comfort on its way. Accept His comfort now, and so prepare for the comfort at hand."[3]

To view the role of pain and suffering properly, one must await the whole story. Promises of it abound in the Bible:

"And the God of all grace, who called you to his eternal glory in Christ, after you have suffered a little while, will himself restore you and make you strong, firm and steadfast" (1 Peter 5:10, NIV). "These troubles and sufferings of ours are, after all, quite small and won't last very long. Yet this short time of distress will result in God's richest blessing upon us forever and ever! So we do not look at what we can see right now, the troubles all around us, but we look forward to the joys in heaven which we have not yet seen. The troubles will soon be over, but the joys to come will last forever" (2 Corinthians 4:17-18, TLB).

Peter and Paul were so confident of the end result that they staked their ministries, their health, their very lives on Christ's promises.

Death and Birth

Ironically, the one event which probably causes more emotional suffering than any other—death—is in reality a translation, a time for great joy when Christ's victory will be appropriated to each of us. Describing the effect of His own death, Jesus used the simile of a woman in labor, travailing until the moment of childbirth when all is replaced by ecstasy (John 16: 21).

Each of our individual deaths can be seen as a birth. Imagine what it would be like if you had had full consciousness as a fetus and could now remember those sensations:

Your world is dark, safe, secure. You are bathed in warm liquid, cushioned from shock. You do nothing for yourself; you are fed automatically, and a murmuring heartbeat assures you that someone larger than you fills all your needs. Your life consists of simple waiting—you're not sure what to wait for, but any change seems far away and scary. You meet no sharp objects, no pain, no threatening adventures. A fine existence.

One day you feel a tug. The walls are falling in on you. Those soft cushions are now pulsing and beating against you, crushing you downwards. Your body is bent double, your limbs twisted and wrenched. You're falling, upside down. For the first time in your life, you feel pain. You're in a sea of roiling matter. There is more pressure, almost too intense to bear. Your head is squeezed flat, and you are pushed harder, harder into a dark tunnel. Oh, the pain. Noise. More pressure.

You hurt all over. You hear a groaning sound and an awful, sudden fear rushes in on you. It is happening—your world is collapsing. You're sure it's the end. You see a piercing, blinding light. Cold, rough hands pull at you. A painful slap. Waaaahhhh!

Congratulations, you have just been born.

Death is like that. On this end of the birth canal, it seems fiercesome, portentous, and full of pain. Death is a scary tunnel and we are being sucked toward it by a powerful force. None of us looks forward to it. We're afraid. It's full of pressure, pain, darkness . . . the unknown. But beyond the darkness and the pain there's a whole new world outside. When we wake up after death in that bright new world, our tears and hurts will be mere memories.[4] And though the new world is so much better than this one, we have no categories to really understand what it will be like. The best the Bible writers can tell us is that then, instead of the silence of God, we will have the presence of God and see Him face-to-face. At that time we will be given a stone, and

18

upon it will be written a new name, which no one else knows. Our birth into new creatures will be complete (Revelation 2:17).

Do you sometimes think God does not hear? That your cries of pain fade into nothing? God is not deaf. He is as grieved by the world's trauma as you are. His only Son died here. But He has promised to set things right. Nothing simply disappears.

Let history finish. Let the symphony scratch out its last mournful note of discord before it bursts into song. As Paul said,

> In my opinion whatever we may have to go through now is less than nothing compared with the magnificent future God has planned for us. The whole creation is on tiptoe to see the wonderful sight of the sons of God coming into their own. . . .
>
> It is plain to anyone with eyes to see that at the present time all created life groans in a sort of universal travail. And it is plain, too, that we who have a foretaste of the Spirit are in a state of painful tension, while we wait for that redemption of our bodies which will mean that at last we have realized our full sonship in him *(Romans 8:18-19, 22-23, Phillips).*

As we look back on the speck of eternity that was the history of this planet, we will be impressed not by its importance, but by its diminutiveness: From the viewpoint of the Andromeda galaxy, the holocaustic destruction of our entire solar system would be barely visible, a match flaring faintly in the distance, then imploding in permanent darkness. Yet for this burnt-out match, God sacrificed himself.

Pain can be seen, as Berkouwer puts it, as the great "not yet" of eternity. It reminds us of where we are, and fans in us a thirst for where we will someday be.

> *At the height of his suffering, Job spoke:*
> *How I wish someone would record what I am saying*
> *Or with a chisel carve my words in stone*
> *and write them so they would last forever.*
> *But I know there is someone in heaven*
> *who will come at last to my defense.*
> *I will see him with my own eyes,*
> *and he will not be a stranger.*
>
> (Job 19:23 ff., *Job for Modern Man*)

I can believe that one day every bruise and every leukemia cell and every embarrassment and every hurt will be set right, and all those grim moments of hoping against hope will be rewarded.

Where Is God when It Hurts?

For a good portion of my life, I shared the viewpoint of those who rail against God for allowing pain. Suffering pressed in too close. I could find no way to rationalize a world as malignant as this one.

As I visited those whose pain far exceeded my own, though, I was surprised by its effects. Suffering was as likely to produce strengthened faith as to sow agnosticism. And as I visited those with Hansen's disease, particularly, I was convinced of the important role of pain in the world.

In one sense, there will be no solution to pain until Jesus returns and re-creates the earth. I am sustained by faith in that great hope. If I did not truly believe that God is a Physician and not a Sadist, and that He "feels in himself the tortured presence of every nerve that lacks its repose," I would immediately abandon all attempts to plumb the mysteries of suffering. My anger about pain has melted mostly for one reason: I have come to know God. He has given me joy and love and happiness and goodness. They have come in flashes, in the midst of my confused, unrighteous world, but their presence has been absolute enough to convince me that my God is worthy of trust. Knowing Him is worth all enduring.

Where does that leave me when I stand next to a hospital bed the next time a close friend gets Hodgkin's disease? After all, this search started at a bedside. It leaves me with a solid faith in a Person which no amount of suffering can erode. And, because Christianity is worked out in a real world among real people, I also need a few reassurances to grasp the role of suffering in the world.

Where is God when it hurts?

He has been there from the beginning, designing a pain system that still, in the midst of a fallen, rebellious world, bears the stamp of His genius and equips us for life on this planet.

He has watched us reflect His image, carving our great works of art, launching mighty adventures, living out this earth in a mixture of pain and pleasure when the two so closely coalesce they sometimes become almost indistinguishable.

He has used pain, even in its grossest forms, to teach us, asking us to let it turn us to Him. He has stooped to conquer.

He has watched this rebellious planet live on, mercifully allowing the human project to continue its self-guided way.

He has let us cry out and echo Job with louder and harsher fits of anger against Him, blaming Him for a world we spoiled.

He has allied himself with the poor and suffering, establishing a kingdom tilted in their favor, which the rich and powerful often shun.

He has promised supernatural strength to nourish our spirit, even if our physical suffering goes unrelieved.

He has joined us. He has hurt and bled and cried and suffered. He has dignified for all time those who suffer by sharing their pain.

He is with us now, ministering to us through His Spirit and through members of His Body who are commissioned to bear us up and relieve our suffering for the sake of the Head.

He is waiting, gathering the armies of good. One day He will unleash them. The world will see one last explosion of pain before the full victory is ushered in. Then, He will create for us a new, incredible world. And pain shall be no more.

Listen, I tell you a mystery: We shall not all sleep, but we shall all be changed—in a flash, in the twinkling of an eye, at the last trumpet. For the trumpet will sound, the dead will be raised imperishable, and we shall be changed. For the perishable must clothe itself with the imperishable, and the mortal with immortality. When the perishable has been clothed with the imperishable, and the mortal with immortality, then the saying that is written will come true: "Death has been swallowed up in victory."

"Where, O death, is your victory?

Where, O death, is your sting?" (1 Corinthians 15: 51-55, NIV).

"A Whole New World Outside," from *Where Is God when It Hurts?* by Philip Yancey. Copyright 1977 by the Zondervan Corporation. Used by permission.

1. Thomas Howard, "On Brazen Heavens," *Christianity Today*, December 7, 1973, pp. 8-11.

2. Ibid., pp. 9-10.

3. George MacDonald, *Life Essential* (Wheaton, Ill.: Harold Shaw Publishers, 1978), p. 54.

4. Joseph Bayly was the essential source for this analogy.

Chapter 3

Question:
Why do good people suffer?

It's No Sin to Be Sick

by E. Margaret Clarkson

*Background Scriptures: Romans 8:12-17;
Hebrews 2:8-9; 11:27; 1 Peter 4:16-19*

A new error is deceiving many Evangelicals and leaving a trail of destruction. Though promoted as truth, it distorts biblical teaching.

The myth is that salvation is accompanied by instant health. Christians experiencing anything less either lack faith, are out of God's will, or maybe are not really Christians.

"Jesus wants you well," is widely preached in place of the biblical call to repentance towards God, faith in the Lord Jesus Christ, and obedience to the leadership of the Holy Spirit. Little heed is paid to the overall teaching of the Scriptures concerning suffering. Usually only a few isolated verses are considered, and those not always in context. Happiness seems to be more important than God's standards of personal holiness.

Miracles are demanded to exorcise every pain. Those who don't experience miracles are frequently looked upon with suspicion by those who do. International telecasts preach the gospel of salvation plus simultaneous healing—or maybe forget about salvation and simply offer healing.

Meanwhile, those who have been led to expect a miracle are shattered when it does not appear. And who can measure the pressures put upon sensitive believers who must live with continuous suffering when pastors or friends glibly tell them that they suffer because of their own unbelief or secret sin?

How well I know! Though I have been a Christian since age 10, I have lived with pain as far back as I can remember—well over 60 years. Illness has been frequent and disruptive. Medical science has been unable to do much more than offer palliative and moral support.

I know the damage done by well-meaning Christians who take it upon themselves to "deal with" others about the "real reasons" for their illness. In my experience, such persons know little about either pain or the Scriptures. They grasp little of God's long-term purposes for His saints and fail to recognize His overruling sovereignty in the lives of His children.

Consciously or unconsciously they seem to equate their good health with spiritual health, even superiority, and correct others accordingly. Many would utterly crumble under a small part of the suffering that their victim may be bearing with faith and fortitude. Yet they quickly saddle an already overborne soul with man-made guilt—a burden harder to bear than suffering itself. Only God can minister to the wounds inflicted by such cruelty. All too well I know their pain and how long it takes them to heal.

What do the Scriptures teach about suffering and healing?

First, suffering, along with evils of every kind, is ours because of man's sin. Pain is no more God's will for man than is death. Both are man's answer to God's gift of free will. Christians have no mandate to isolate illness and seek to exorcise it from our lives as if it were the ultimate evil. We are to war on all sin's

24

anomalies. To focus our efforts unduly on one is to ignore others equally if not more important; and herein lies spiritual peril.

Second, the Scriptures nowhere promise God's children immunity from suffering. Evils come upon Christian and non-Christian alike—and this includes pain. Moreover, the Bible specifically states that suffering here and glory hereafter is the hallmark of Christ's kingdom (Romans 8:17). This is the path marked out by the Captain of our salvation, and if we are true disciples it will be ours as well.

From start to finish the Bible illustrates this principle, and church history bears it out. Every faithful Christian endures suffering of one kind or another (2 Timothy 3:2; 1 Peter 4:16-19; 5:10). Some are bound to experience this as physical illness.

Third, the Scriptures clearly teach that God is sovereign. His purposes will ultimately be fulfilled. That which we now see only dimly will one day shine in everlasting splendor. "Now we see not yet all things put under him. But we see Jesus . . .

crowned with glory and honour"; and so we "endure as seeing him who is invisible" (Hebrews 2:8-9; 11:27). This hope uplifts suffering Christians.

Fourth, God has promised to sustain us in our sufferings, not necessarily to deliver us out of them. God did not spare His beloved Son; He does not always spare His human children either. Rather than sending deliverance, sometimes His "way to escape" (1 Corinthians 10:13) turns out to be His enabling to bear the pain.

Fifth, suffering may be designed to bring glory to God. Job, an innocent, God-fearing man, was allowed to suffer horribly and without explanation in order that God's power might be vindicated before Satan.

The man born blind (John 9) endured years of darkness before Jesus demonstrated His power to give both physical and spiritual sight—and forever settled the question of suffering being punishment for personal sin. Lazarus was allowed to die and his sisters to suffer grief (John 11) that Christ's power over death might be displayed. The list of those called to suffer for God's glory does not end with the biblical story—it extends to this day.

Finally, God uses suffering to reveal himself to us. Job's faithfulness was rewarded by an experience of God far exceeding anything known in his day. Long before Abraham, Job glimpsed immortality and bodily resurrection.

When the Pharisees cast out the man born blind, Jesus sought him out and revealed himself as Son of God. To Lazarus He revealed himself as the Overcomer of death.

Multiplied thousands from that day to this have come to thank God for the pain that brought them a personal vision of God. I am one of these. I have experienced God more through pain than in any other way. Naturally I should prefer to come to know Him apart from suffering. But the important thing is to know Him. Knowledge of himself is His special gift to those who suffer in the will of God.

What about healing? Those whose view of suffering is truly biblical are unlikely to have difficulty about healing.

God both can and does heal. Both the Old and New Testaments teach this. In general, biblical miracles marked the beginning of a new era by significant signs and wonders. So we see Him as God the Father in His miraculous care of the emerging nation of Israel. We see Him as God the Son in the miracles of Jesus, and as God the Holy Spirit in the miracles of the Early Church.

Other than in these historic clusters, recorded miracles seem to have been infrequent and to have occurred in more or less isolated instances.

The gifts of the Spirit given at Pentecost have never been withdrawn. Subject to God's sovereign choice, they are operative today. This includes the gift of healing. No suffering Christian should fail to seek healing from God, though he should recognize that God works today through medicine, surgery, psychiatry, nursing, and physical or other therapy more often than He does by divine intervention. God is the source of all healing; we must allow Him to work by whatever means He may choose.

We cannot demand healing. God has not promised to heal every ailing Christian. Some He heals; others, like Paul who sought healing three times, He refuses for His own inscrutable reasons. The biblical Christian is willing to accept God's answer, yes or no. If he is healed, he gives glory to God.

Reprinted from *Moody Monthly*. Used by permission.

Chapter 4

Where Was God when I Needed Him?

by Al Truesdale

*Background Scriptures: Romans 8:35-39;
Hebrews 13:20-21*

The *Kansas City Star* shouted this question at me from the front page of the Thursday evening edition. Prominently displayed was a picture of 53-year-old James Wheat, sitting outside his charred home that had been destroyed by fire the night before. He was unemployed, the father of a 15-year-old son. Seven months earlier his wife had died of a heart attack. "My son," Wheat said, "is about to lose his mind worrying about me." Choking back tears, Wheat told Dorothy Gast, the *Star* reporter, "I used to go to church, but where was God when I needed Him? It looks like I'm being punished, but I don't know why. Everything I've ever worked for is gone." He added, "I go looking, but I can't find a job. They say I'm too old. But I can work as well as anyone. All I need is a job."

Immediately below this story was the picture of Eric Harris, a professional football player drafted by the Kansas City Chiefs of the National Football League. At that time Eric Harris had not reported to training camp, and had refused to sign a contract to play with the Chiefs. Why? Because he and the Chiefs were at odds over the terms of his $1.14 million contract offer.

One man, one human being created in God's image, weeps because he cannot find a job to feed himself and his 15-year-old son, while another complains about the terms of a $1.14 million contract.

Perhaps you have an illustration of this question that is more striking than mine. Perhaps you are that illustration!

Why is life not fair?

This is one of mankind's most persistent and perplexing questions. It is as ancient as it is modern. It has been asked by cultures and religions in all parts of the world, by the Egyptians in the third millennium B.C., and by the Babylonians in the second. The Greeks, 800 years before Christ, answered the question according to their understanding of the activities of such gods as Zeus, Apollo, and Pluto. The Greek tragedeans wrote about the disasters that happen to people, especially kings and heroic warriors. But they were not always clear why the gods visited such evils on man—were they distributing justice fairly or were they acting from sheer willfulness?

The ancient Hindus, hundreds of years before the birth of Christ, thought that life's misfortunes came from Rudra, the storm god, destroyer of goods and persons. Their successors, and other religions that had their origin in India, believed that the conditions encountered in this life are the direct result of the law of Karma, the impersonal law in the universe that supposedly sets the conditions of this life according to how a person lived in a prior one.

The Taoists (Dowists) of ancient China believed that since we can never be sure that our misfortunes will not in fact turn out to be blessings, we should not fret about anything that happens to us. Accept everything as coming from the eternal Tao and be at peace with the world.

Others in our own time teach that pain and sorrow are only illusions, that what we need is simply a better way of viewing life. They believe, for example, that pain is unreal. They are confident that freedom from what we perceive to be pain can be gained by the mind's conquest over this illusion.

But for Christians who worship the God who is the Father of our Lord, these answers are unacceptable. The Bible is witness to this as God proclaims that He is the Creator of heaven and earth, that He is its loving Governor, and that He wills His best for it. It is precisely this affirmation, this knowledge, that intensifies the sting in the question, "Why is life not fair?" If this kind of God controls the world, why is life not more equitable? Why do the events of life so often appear to be completely out of control?

Perhaps surprisingly to some, the Bible which contains the great affirmations about God's love and care for us also contains candid and penetrating challenges to the truthfulness of these affirmations. Three such challenges may be found in the books of Job, Habakkuk, and Ecclesiastes. In each, the question is asked, "How, in the face of what appears to be strong evidence to the contrary, can faith in the wisdom and goodness of God be sustained?"

Why is life unfair? Let us look at some possible answers to this question.

1. First, we should be willing to honestly ask, "Am I the cause of what I now perceive to be the unfair circumstances of my life?" Or, if someone else seems to be the victim of injustice, the same question should be asked about them. This may appear to be a cruel question. It is not meant to be. The fact is, however, that until we face this question, any answer will probably be unrealistic, deceptive, and temporary at best. I must ask if my problem or my neighbor's plight is the product of one or a series of unwise decisions about the course of life's directions. Was timely medical care refused, money unwisely spent or invested, a hasty or ill-advised choice of a husband or wife made, educational opportunities squandered, or character development left unattended?

The list of questions could continue. "To answer the question, 'Why is life not fair?'" my friend says, "most of us don't have to look any further than the end of our noses." Some people deal very unfairly with God and with life. They neither plan to succeed in life, nor do they commit the necessary energy to the discipline that orderly and fruitful life requires. The emphysema victim who, contrary to his doctor's advice, has been a heavy smoker for 40 years, is not being fair when he asks, "How could God allow me to die in this condition?" A young couple, both of whom dropped out of school at age 16, struggles from week to week, barely able to feed and clothe themselves and their three children. They left school in order to "start making money and get the things they wanted." Should they be surprised that in our highly technological society such a lack of preparation for life is rarely rewarded with social and financial security?

I have met people who blame God, or the devil, for failures and tragedies that should be properly attributed to their own carelessness. It is neither God's nor the devil's fault that on a hot July day a mother left a one-year-old child unattended in an automobile to go into a drug store to shop. Responsibility for the child's suffocation was hers.

2. *Perhaps life is not really as unfair as it seems.* Upon reflection, most of us would admit that we tend to assess misfortunes in life as much worse than they actually are. This is not surprising, however. When buffeted by life's adverse experiences, we usually lack the necessary perspective for taking their true measure. We are not able to see things in the broad context as God sees them, and our responses are usually governed by our limited approval. Which of us, when time has expanded our understanding, has not looked back on an undesirable experience and said, "That really wasn't as bad as it seemed at the time"?

It is also true, as most of us have experienced, that many things in life which at first appear to be devastating misfortunes are actually transformed into significant benefits for us. The perceived misfortunes turned out to be the necessary first steps in the transformation.

31

3. But if adverse experiences may not be as devastating and unfair as they seem, *it may also be true that matters are not nearly so well with other people as we judge them to be.* In other words, if facts were known, perhaps the person we think has received more than his share of good things, but whose style of life is anything but a credit, may have suffered in ways that would shame us for our thoughts. That person whose furnace, we are sure, never goes on the blink when income taxes are due, whose children never contract appendicitis at two o'clock in the morning, or who never suffers the fear and embarrassment of domestic turmoil, the devastating pain of grief, or financial loss, may in fact carry within him a reservoir of sorrow beside which our misfortunes pale to insignificance.

Most people, it seems, have learned to suffer quietly. In some respects, our culture demands this. But most of us have occasions of astonishment upon learning that a neighbor, a colleague, a client, or a relative has suffered a business failure, an illness, or a death that would have ruined us. Which of us has not whispered, "O God, please forgive me for the times I complained over little things"?

4. *But even when these qualifications are made, there are still many instances in which life does seem to be unfair,* when innocent parties are victimized by circumstances or people over whom they have little or no control. Or, there are situations where poor choices were made in the past, but where the dividends of sorrow and pain paid, now far exceed the limits of sanity and justice. In times like these a strong, anguished moral protest against the oppressive imbalance of things escapes our lips.

The Spanish artist, Picasso, captured on canvas the moral energy of this outrage and horror in the faces of Spanish peasants who were victims of the Spanish Civil War. Defenseless, they were being mercilessly bombed by Nazi aircraft. Which of us has not felt this moral outrage when viewing pictures of Jews being led to Hitler's gas chambers, or when viewing the X rays of a child's mangled body, the victim of a father's drunken anger?

After 14 years I am still incensed over the loss of a friend, the gifted wife of a district superintendent, whose radiant life was viciously snuffed out in a head-on collision with an automobile driven by a drunken youth. The list of such unjustices is almost endless. In most of these, try as we may, we can distill absolutely no benefits from them. It is precisely their senselessness that provokes our revolt.

5. Another part of the answer to our question, "Why is life not fair?" is *the simple and stark fact, "because that's just the way life is."* Now, before we recoil at what seems to be resignation in the face of fate, let us admit that in a world as complex as ours, where there are so many competing interests among so many people, a perfect balance of all goods and evils is, although imaginable, highly unrealistic.

The principle of cause and effect operates in the world of nature and in society. Its suspension in the interest of eliminating all undesirable effects that result from its operation could not be achieved without also eliminating all prospects of its desirable benefits. The world operates in a dependable way according to what we call "the laws of nature." These "laws" make normal living possible. One of the laws of nature is friction, that phenomenon that keeps the wheels of the car from spinning fruitlessly and makes forward progress possible. That law will allow a person to be killed in an automobile that is traveling too fast for road conditions. It also enables the farmer to pull equipment to plant in the spring and harvest an abundant yield in the fall.

The desire to put life in order, to arrange and balance its elements in some more or less predictable and equitable manner, is a noble human sentiment. But the fact remains that there are many things over which we exercise no control. Unexpected and harsh events occur that scorn our efforts to derive from them any sense of purpose or order. Facing this realistically is a vital part of human maturity. This does not make life's "unfair experiences" any more pleasant, but it can help us maintain our equilibrium in the midst of them.

6. *We need to emphasize that there are many people who suffer very real injustices for which none of the above suggested answers provide an adequate solution.* A 19-year-old mother is

unable to find emotional and sexual fulfillment in marriage because from age 6 until she left home at age 16 she was habitually molested by her father. She won't be comforted by the answer, "That's just the way life is!" She knows full well that for most people life isn't that way at all.

7. *As Christians, the most important response to our question has to be found in the love that God has expressed toward us in our Lord, Jesus Christ.*

The Bible, and more specifically the New Testament, does not dodge the unfair character of life, nor the pain and disappointment it generates. Our Lord himself was the victim of gross injustice. But it does say that for us the inequities of life do not have the last word about our peace or welfare. The inequities of life are not finally of ultimate importance. The Christian's foundation for happiness or blessedness does not depend on how balanced life is, but on the fact that in Christ, God has joined himself to us with a redemptive, creative, and sustaining love that nothing in life can dismantle. Hear the words of Paul,

> Who shall separate us from the love of Christ? Shall trouble or hardship or persecution or famine or nakedness or danger or sword? As it is written: "For your sake we face death all day long; we are considered as sheep to be slaughtered." No, in all these things we are more than conquerors through him who loved us. For I am convinced that neither death nor life, neither angels nor demons, neither the present nor the future, nor any powers, either height nor depth, nor anything else in all creation, will be able to separate us from the love of God that is in Christ Jesus our Lord *(Romans 8:35-39, NIV)*.

The Psalms also proclaim the faithfulness of God, the unfailing source of peace and fortitude amid life's storms. The 23rd psalm is an excellent example.

For a young community of Christians buffetted by persecution, the writer to the Hebrews prayed, "May the God of peace, who brought again from the dead our Lord Jesus, the great shepherd of the sheep, by the blood of the eternal covenant, equip you with everything good that you may do his will, working

34

in you that which is pleasing in his sight, through Jesus Christ; to whom be glory forever and ever, Amen" (Hebrews 13:20-21, RSV).

The peace of God. This is the Christian's anchor in life.

What is this peace? It is the presence of Christ in us, the One who has triumphed over every foe that would deprive us of God's peace. Through the Holy Spirit He cultivates this peace in us. Paul's prayer for the Ephesians is an excellent expression of Christ's promise to us. "I pray that out of his glorious riches he may strengthen you with power through his Spirit in your inner being, so that Christ may dwell in your hearts through faith" (Ephesians 3:16, NIV).

In one of the great New Testament anthems Paul says, "Blessed be the God and Father of our Lord Jesus Christ, the Father of mercies and God of all comfort, who comforts us in all our affliction so that we may be able to comfort those who are in any affliction with the comfort with which we ourselves are comforted by God" (2 Corinthians 1:3-4, RSV). Thus the most important factor in the Christian's life is not whether life is fair, but that life's inequities cannot separate us from the "God of all comfort, who comforts us in all our affliction" (v. 3).

Anyone who does not have this hope and comfort must insist that life be fair. He or she must expend emotional and physical energy insisting that life be fair because beyond this elusive hope there is nothing more to which they can appeal. Christians who live this way have not yet understood the deeper meaning of faith in God.

After realizing that his "thorn in the flesh" would stay with him, Paul experienced in a new way the source of Christian stability and purpose, "My grace is sufficient for you, for my power is made perfect in weakness" (2 Corinthians 12:9, RSV).

There is one other very important factor that should govern the way Christians face the inequities of life: the hope of Christ's coming and the expectation of that great day when the all-wise God will make all things right. The words given to the apostle John, himself a victim of injustice, are also meant for you.

Then I saw a new heaven and a new earth, for the first heaven and the first earth had passed away, and there was no longer any sea. I saw the Holy City, the new Jerusalem, coming down out of heaven from God, prepared as a bride beautifully dressed for her husband. And I heard a loud voice from the throne saying, "Now the dwelling of God is with men, and he will live with them. They will be his people, and God himself will be with them and be their God. He will wipe every tear from their eyes. There will be no more death or mourning or crying or pain, for the old order of things has passed away *(Revelation 21:1-4, NIV)*.

But this does not mean that Christians should simply resign as passive victims to all life's misfortunes. In many instances there are ways to improve on bad situations, to overcome injustices, to convert liabilities into assets, and to reverse what appear to be hopeless defeats. True, for the Christian, peace and hope do not depend on how smooth the waters of life are. But, it is also true that with God's help many of the storms can be stilled, or at least minimized, and the ship of life set on course again.

We should learn to look for creative ways to resolve problems that appear to have beaten us. Many are the biographies, written and unwritten, of people who have refused to surrender to the defeat heaped on them. One inspiring example in our time was Helen Keller.

A friend of mine has been blind since he was a teenager. However, he did not allow this to make him a sullen and self-pitying person. Instead, he dreamed of what he could do and he set out to bring these dreams to realization. He is one of the most radiant people I know. He now has a Ph.D. in English literature from the University of Georgia, is a college professor, frightens most chess players because of his stunning ability to win, and loves to relax in the evening by playing Beethoven on his violin.

"Your life certainly will be colored by this awful accident," a visitor said to the young lady whose body had been disfigured in an automobile accident brought on by the drunken driver of the other auto. "Yes," she replied, "and with God's help I intend to choose the colors."

36

Chapter 5

Question: **Why is there strife and war?**

The Savagery of Man

by Leonard W. Dodson
Chaplain, U.S. Navy

Background Scriptures

War   *Psalms 55:21; 120; Isaiah 2:4; 2 Corinthians 10:3-5; 1 Peter 2:11*

Strife   *Psalm 55:9; Proverbs 15:18; 29:22; Romans 13:12-14; 1 Corinthians 3:3; 1 Timothy 6: 3-4; James 3:14, 16; Proverbs 10:12; 2 Corinthians 12:20; Ephesians 6:11-17*

For almost 30 years I have lived and ministered in a military environment. I have watched the evolution of the instruments of war from fairly simple systems to the most complex. The advent of the nuclear age has thrust all of mankind into a new posture of survival. The United States is just one among the nuclear powers, yet it, alone, has enough destructive force to destroy every living thing on earth 10 times! On a scale of comparison, the atom bomb of Hiroshima would be one-half inch high; in proportion, our new thermo-nuclear bomb would be 128 miles high on a graph of destructive power! The polarity of the super powers, indeed, makes this a dangerous world.

The "balance of power" has characterized the nuclear age, of *mutual assured destruction*—MAD, what a descriptive acronym! As soon as there is excessive disparity in strength, either between individuals or nations, the risk of conflict appears. Either the weaker party is threatened to be crushed, or he will rebel against the superior. Perceived weakness, in relationship to the accelerating power of one's adversary, invites the "first strike" before the gap widens. Such a confrontation is unthinkable if civilization, as we know it, is to survive. The balance of power is always in danger of becoming a test of strength and will.

When these "unthinkable thoughts" crowd in on us, we are overwhelmed with anxiety. Some psychologists have told us that the prospect of global annihilation hanging over our heads, like Damocles' sword, produced the aberrant behavior of the 50s and 60s. The 70s descended into an anxious time of despair, stress, and hopelessness. In today's secular environment, it is difficult to find an optimist. The expansionist enthusiasm of the American dream has been subsumed into an attitude of retrenchment, conservation, and pessimism.

One does not need to confine his observations to the military. In the civilian sector of society, strife and violence characterize mass-media presentations and interpersonal relationships. A sampling of the morning news brings charges of police brutality against District of Columbia police in the arrest of almost 200 demonstrators. I watched the expression and heard the cacophony of voices from the observers urging the police to "kill them—send them back where they belong!" The morning paper noted that one adjacent county had five murders the first 20 days of the month while our own only had four! A TV program examined professional wrestling. They focused on the crowd. The expressions of hate—watching the voice of violence was disturbing. A normal evening of TV watching reveals the savagery that is basic to current video programing. Recent studies of violence in the home and family revealed that it has per-

38

meated the warp and woof of our society. The physical abuse of children and wives is increasing at such an alarming rate as to rouse national concern.

Miami's Liberty City, Chattanooga, Detroit, Watts, Washington, D.C., all were recent scenes of racial violence and destruction. The Emancipation Proclamation gave freedom to Black American slaves, the Civil Rights Act of 1954 guaranteed civil rights for all citizens, but it has not stopped the violence and conflict between the races. What has happened to the human race? Why are we a violent people?

Perhaps we should provide a working definition of what we mean by war and strife. The American Heritage Dictionary defines *war* as, "A state of open armed, often prolonged conflicts carried on between nations, states, or parties. Any condition of active antagonisms or contention." *Strife* is defined as, "Heated, often violent dissention; bitter conflict. A contention; struggle between rivals."

The Scriptures portray war as a state of hostility between nations, states, provinces, or individuals. In 2 Corinthians the apostle Paul puts it in a spiritual sense by saying "we do not war after the flesh" (2 Corinthians 10:3). The Old Testament portrays war in its brutality. The Hebrews distinguished between two kinds of wars: some were ordered by God and were an obligation; others were voluntary, launched by leaders for their own purposes. I have heard war defended and justified by Old Testament quotes and then condemned by quotes from the New Testament. Is the Bible contradictory in regards to war or is there a clear scriptural teaching that provides guidelines for our generation?

There is no easy, pat answer. A mere yes or no in response to the morality of the question, evades the larger issue of this chapter, and that is the *why?*

There is no answer from law—international, national, or civil. Societies create laws for their own purposes. All conflict conforms to a pattern. There is always the privileged party, standing on and enforcing the laws that benefit them in the exercise of their power. In war, every government declares the rightness of their cause and the imperative for victory. They consistently transfer the blame for the conflict to the enemy. Nations, in order to preserve themselves, authorize their citizens to destroy human life when it is the enemy and reward them for doing so, while upholding the sacredness of human life within their own society. This violence is always justified in the eyes of those who see themselves as being "in the right." Power is gained by violence, and the violence is justified by power. Power becomes the supreme value.

Violence and conflict erupt as soon as one person, or community, claims to be the sole custodian of the truth. There is nothing that gives such feeling of exhilaration as the certainty that you possess truth. It is dangerous for men and nations, not so much to be right, as to be absolutely sure that they are right. Law, then, becomes nothing more than a resource to violence to combat violence. The very essence of a viscious circle.

We are all against violence. We all condemn it and we all have a certain respect for it. Our national holidays are often celebrations of violence. The real problem is how to decide whether an act of violence is justified or not. Everyone recognizes that there is a violence which is necessary to resist culpable violence. It is a violence organized by society, with its police, courts, and military, in order to stop brutal force from triumphing and destroying the life of the community. Criminal violence is outlawed; punitive violence is written into the law.

Legal violence invites retaliation. Violence carries within itself a dynamic of growth which insures that it will increase. It can trigger a chain reaction. The law does not solve the problem of violence, it only confines itself to preserving its own from its worst effects. Disorder soon appears where power is lacking. Men and nations revert to the "law of the jungle" as soon as the restraining influences of forces of "law and order" are removed. It is evident, then, that some violence, within the law, regulates society. It sets limits to savagery. Consensus demands that we live within those limits. When those boundaries are ignored there is conflict and war. While it is impossible within the length of this chapter to deal with the problem in depth, we have taken another step closer to the awesome question, "Why is there strife and war?"

I would like to place this in the polarity of two philosophical positions which, if one is correct, then of necessity, the other is wrong. It is the most important conceptual confrontation of our day. It is the face-down of humanism, as an explanation of man and his environment, and the Christian view of man. If the humanist is correct, even the ethical humanist, then the secular, pluralistic world is all that exists.

The Pythagorean principle that man is the measure of all things, is the basic value upon which the humanist builds. It assumes that there is no eternal objective value system that orders, directs, and then judges men's actions and lives. The existentialist is correct in saying that there are no "givens," all is relative. Life's highest good becomes subjective—based entirely on the principle of pleasure/pain is wrong. The "now generation" is consistently living out this value system. "Why get married?" they ask, the vows are just words. It is how we "feel" about each other that matters. A piece of paper will not make it valid. What happens to the relationship when feelings change? Persons in this kind of a relationship are part of the throw-away products of a consumer society.

What a difference in contrast to Christian marriage, "For this reason one forsakes father and mother . . . and cleaves to another . . . through sickness, health, until death parts," in the words of the ancient ritual.

Why work? It is a hassle to join the "rat race" and support the establishment. It is much more enjoyable to drop out, enjoy the food stamps, hitch rides in air-conditioned cars, and use free medical clinics that the establishment provides, than to feel that all we do, "we do as unto the Lord."

Why pursue an education? It is only a cultural trap to confine one to society's expectations.

No, humanism tells me to be free, to do my own thing, that I alone am the judge of what is right or wrong. No one can lay his "trip" on me. Is it any wonder we have developed the drug culture, social sex, open marriage, a sensual society? No wonder there is a breakdown in interpersonal relationships, family structures, societal mores, and value systems that impose limits. This brand of spurious freedom ignores limits and declares its own autonomous independence. It demands independence from God, society, the church, and all external authority. If carried to its logical extreme, it leads back to the law of the jungle, that is, survival of the fittest, to a violent world where one must constantly protect oneself from being destroyed. The final conclusion is chaos, man alienated from God, from himself, and from others. No wonder man feels abandoned and alone. Humanism says that this world is all there is—there is no God, no judgment, no eternity. Just threescore years and ten. No wonder the suicide rate (self-imposed violence) is so high among those generations, educationally and culturally conditioned by this philosophy. As one young adult summed it up for me, "Life is a drag!" When you take away the sacred beliefs that bring cohesion to society, there is always disarray and chaos.

Fyodor Dostoyevski says in his novel *Possessed,* "If God does not exist then everything is permissible." Ah, there it is again, the spiritual dimension that brings me face-to-face with God. If God is, then I must do business with Him. The Bible asserts that God is the Creator of nature and of man. Man is to have mastery over nature, tend it, and preserve it. What God forbids for man to do is to elevate himself, to be the sole judge of what is good and what is evil. That is the province of God.

Man's power comes from God. As soon as man thinks he is all-powerful he abuses that privilege and imposes his will on others. The root of the problem of violence, that produces strife and war, is the problem of evil. Jesus tells us in Matthew 7:17, "Every good tree bears good fruit, but a bad tree bears bad fruit" (NIV).

Essential problems are not about methods but about values; not about functions but about persons. Persons can never be reduced to an inventory of functions. Ever since Cain and Abel, man has been obsessed with exterminating his rival. Rousseau sees man as good by nature and that he is preserved from the worst effects of his violence by society. He sees man as he is and as the Bible shows him to be. Romans 3:10 tells us that sin-sickness is a congenital disease which man does not contract by accident, but receives it as he receives his physical

42

life. This problem of evil in man is revealed from the third chapter of Genesis throughout the Bible. This evil comes as a loss of limits. The Fall and expulsion from the Garden is the result of man's challenge to the God-imposed limits.

Man, created in the image and likeness of God, stepped over the limits of freedom given by God and has plunged himself into alienation, rebellion, and conflict ever since. He feels guilty because he is guilty. He feels alone because he is alienated from his Creator. He cannot relate to his fellowman in harmony and peace because he is at war within himself. Because he violated the limits of freedom, he no longer knows what freedom means. When he tries to liberate others he brings instead, war, destruction, and death. Since he is adrift, cut loose from his spiritual, moral, and ethical moorings, he is anxious and alone. His life is one of chaos. But as God in Genesis 1:1 spoke order out of chaos, only God can bring order once more to the disorder and disarray of the individual life.

Basically, we face a choice of faith. Man needs and seeks order in his life. The secure, structured existence he seeks is unrealistic. Only a faith that looks to God and His eternal plan and purpose can satisfy the human quest. The security man seeks comes only from the outside transcendent source. It is a faith rooted in trust in God's promises. This trust requires transformation. It must transcend the past, grope its way through the changes of the present, and embrace with hope the future God has planned. It is based on the confidence that God is still God, that He is in control and will have the final word in respect to His universe and man. The kingdoms of this world will indeed become the kingdom of our God and of His Christ.

There must be a belief in the sovereignty of God. The antithesis of this world is One who is greater than this world. The Bible does not evade or sidestep this flaw in nature, or in man. It speaks plainly about the need for redemption and restoration. Jesus promised that man would be saved from his sins; the flawed nature cleansed and restored. But it took death on a Cross to accomplish it. The violence in man was focused on the perfect Man, the God-Man, Christ Jesus. He became the perfect sacrifice, the divine intervention. He alone is capable of restoring man to God's purpose.

But man can accept that divine intervention or reject it. Our sense of sin is linked to freedom of choice. Sin, then, is a matter of the will, or choice. Unregenerated, we go on making these choices with a broken, flawed, sin-twisted will. God has given us that much freedom. By faith man sees that Christ alone can transform the human heart from which wars and strife are launched. "From whence come wars and fightings among you. Come they not hence, even of your lusts that war in your members? Ye fight and war yet ye have not, because ye ask not. Ye ask, and receive not, because ye ask amiss, that ye may consume it upon your lusts" (James 4:1-3). Man walks by faith, some kind of faith in something or someone. Faith in Christ is a realistic faith. Faith does not give us reasons for the tragedy of sin that has destroyed God's perfect plan for His world and for man.

It gives us power to meet it and transform it by grace through faith in Jesus Christ. "For though we walk in the flesh, we do not war after the flesh; (For the weapons of our warfare are not carnal, but mighty through God to the pulling down of strong holds;) Casting down imaginations, and every high thing that exalteth itself against the knowledge of God and bringing into captivity every thought to the obedience of Christ" (2 Corinthians 10:3-5).

Modern man struggles with his guilt. This produces the conflict between persons, society, and nations. When we banish God from our world we become persons ruled by fear. Harold Urey, Nobel Prize winner in chemistry, was one of the physicists who developed the atom bomb. He said, "I write to make you afraid. I myself am a man who is afraid. All the wise men I know are afraid." Ever since man has banished God he is afraid, having lost his sense of God-given identity. Personal disorder has always produced public disorder. Change the individual and thereby change society. Unless the world returns to moral and spiritual values affirming the validity of the spirit, destructive power will continue to rule. "Abstain from sinful desires, which war against your soul" (1 Peter 2:11, NIV).

Summary

The Scriptures are honest and realistic in showing us the origin of strife and war. They arise from the fall of man, vividly portraying the flawed and the brokenness of our world. The apostle Paul states that the entire creation groans for that day of redemption. The fact of sin is evident both in nature and in man. The evil nature of man produces evil acts. As a good tree brings forth good fruit, so an evil tree brings forth corrupt fruit. War is not a good and cannot be justified as such. It has its origins in the degenerate heart of man. Strife between persons is as old as fallen man. Cain killed Abel and man has been cast in an adversary role seeking to destroy his rivals ever since. Man has fallen, nature is flawed, but this does not mean that the divine intervention of God has been thwarted. He provides a perfect sacrifice for sin through the God-Man, Jesus Christ. Through Him, there is the possibility, based on man's choice and acceptance of regeneration, of new spiritual life and restoration as sons of God. Paul tells us, "That if any man be in Christ Jesus he is a new creature: old things are passed away; behold, all things are become new" (2 Corinthians 5:17). Man regenerated, reborn, is the answer to strife and war.

Why is there strife and war? Because man is sinful and the natural fruits of sin are sinful acts and attitudes that lead to strife and war. Whatever lofty view of man the humanist may seek to offer, the fact remains that man is still a sinner outside of Jesus Christ. When Jesus Christ comes into our lives, in response to our faith, He gives us a new nature, a new life. Sin is removed as far as the east is from the west and buried in the sea of divine forgetfulness to be remembered against us no more, forever. We are new creatures with a new nature bringing forth the fruits of the Spirit which are, "love, joy, peace, long-suffering, gentleness, goodness, faith, meekness, temperance" (Galatians 5:22-23).

When our life is hid in Christ we become our brother's keeper and live in harmony and peace with one another. "The night is far spent, the day is at hand: let us therefore cast off the works of darkness, and let us put on the armour of light. Let us walk honestly, as in the day; not in rioting and drunkenness, not in chambering and wantonness, not in strife and envying. But put ye on the Lord Jesus Christ, and make not provision for the flesh, to fulfil the lusts thereof" (Romans 13:12-14). When that happens, the golden rule will work. We will love our neighbor as ourself. We will reflect the love of God through Jesus Christ, witnessed to by the Holy Spirit.

Society will be redeemed only as men are redeemed. The will of God shall be done on earth as it is in heaven only as individuals surrender to the will of God in their lives and follow in obedience. If evil comes from the heart of unregenerate man, then righteousness can only come from the heart of righteous man, redeemed and cleansed through the blood of Jesus Christ.

> Put on the whole armour of God, that ye may be able to stand against the wiles of the devil. For we wrestle not against flesh and blood, but against principalities, against powers, against the rulers of the darkness of this world, against spiritual wickedness in high places. Wherefore take unto you the whole armour of God, that ye may be able to withstand in the evil day, and having done all, to stand. Stand therefore, having on the breastplate of righteousness; and your feet shod with the preparation of the gospel of peace; above all, taking the shield of faith, wherewith ye shall be able to quench all the fiery darts of the wicked. And take the helmet of salvation, and the sword of the Spirit, which is the word of God *(Ephesians 6:11-17)*.

Change man and thereby change the world. Let the spiritual warfare within the person find its perfect peace in Jesus Christ and we can then beat our swords into plowshares. "And he shall judge among the nations, and shall rebuke many people: and they shall beat their swords into plowshares, and their spears into pruninghooks: nation shall not lift up sword against nation, neither shall they learn war anymore" (Isaiah 2:4).

Is it any wonder Jesus told us to go into all the world and preach the gospel to every creature. Mankind's illness is a universal sickness and needs a message of universal effectiveness to cure the sickness of sin. Jesus Christ alone is the Way, the Truth, and the Life. No man can come to God except through Him and as the Holy Spirit draws him. If you want a peaceful world, transform men through the peace of God that passes all understanding. "Thou wilt keep him in perfect peace, whose mind is stayed on thee" (Isaiah 26:3).

Question:
**How can we reconcile a God of
love with a belief in hell?**

The Dark Side of Love

by Clayton Bonar

*Background Scriptures: Luke 12:5; John 3:16-17;
Romans 5:12, 18*

Grasping the subject of this chapter is somewhat like
taking hold of the horns of a bull without giving due regard for
the rest of the critter. A well-rounded study would need to give
some attention to such themes as sin, wrath, judgment, atone-
ment, confession, and forgiveness. Nevertheless, we shall
endeavor to clarify some of the basic issues in order that proper
conclusions can be drawn from them.

Clearing Up Some Misconceptions

First it is vital to our discussion to note that the term
love is not developed in isolation among the biblical writers. Just
as surely as John records "God is love" (1 John 4:8), God
responds in scripture, "I am holy" (Leviticus 11:44; 1 Peter
1:15-16). This is the balance of the Bible. Any study of God's
love which omits His holiness suffers in the process. Thus, it is a
holy love which seeks us out.

A portion of Michelangelo's "Last Judgment" fresco in the
Sistine Chapel, the Vatican.

To make this distinction is to destroy the soft concepts of a
sentimental love so popular today. This new perception will
control one's views of our Lord's other responses to man. God's
love reaches us where we are. God's holiness reaches out with
quite specific expectations about our continued relationship with
Him. It is at this point God brings both His grace and judgment
to the world; grace to receive the penitent heart and judgment
against the rebellious soul.

The **second** help toward a proper understanding of God's
love is to warn against any perception of hell as a part of God's
grand scheme of creation. His attitude toward this place of
horror is not the same as His attitude toward, say, the created
universe. Genesis, chapter one, describes the rest of God's

creation as a result of divine favor. But hell was the consequence of judgment against rebellion in heaven (Matthew 25: 41). On this verse Wesley comments, "Not originally for you; you are intruders into everlasting fire."[1]

Third, the popular expression of this place of torment in Dante's epic poem is not biblically accurate. In the poem, *The Divine Comedy,* hell is described as a multistoried pit of torture. Beyond the gates, in Dante's vision, lies the kingdom of sorrows. It appears to be a place where Satan heaps his demonic vengeance upon those poor, helpless souls so unfortunate as to fall eternally into his grasp.

The Bible makes it clear, though, that Satan does not reign over this kingdom as if it were a satisfactory alternative to what he originally wished for—equality with God while reigning in heaven. It is the last and eternal place of judgment for this rebel spirit and his fallen angels.

Man's Lost Estate

Hell also becomes the judgment of God upon the sinner. God created man for himself. The story of creation is clear as to God's lovely intentions for His new "man." This can be found in the first chapter of Genesis. In fellowship with God, a man was to be the earthly representative for a heavenly design. He was made in the image of God, his Creator.

Chapter three of Genesis records the fall of man. His seduction by the serpent placed the judgment of God upon him. The Bible confirms this judgment. One such indictment is from the pen of Paul to the Christians in Rome, "Wherefore, as by one man sin entered into the world, and death by sin; and so death passed upon all men, for that all have sinned" (Romans 5:12). Man is out of bounds now. He was made for fellowship with God and is separated from Him by sin. Unless there is a redemptive remedy, he suffers the judgment of Satan upon him.

Many of the people in this generation have conferred deity upon themselves, presuming that the world came into being for their convenience. This modern form of "practical atheism" has shifted the throne room of the universe from heaven to earth. Men would like to be rulers in order to rewrite the moral laws on which the universe was founded by the Creator. If they could successfully deny the existence of the sovereign God, or disregard Him as they would a senile old man, then life would be radically different. They could, to use the old saying, sow their wild oats and pray for a crop failure. Or, even better, they could insist that a "loving God" change the rules at their behest so that they would never have to experience the inevitable result of their sinful action.

But God is God and He will not abdicate His sovereign authority for the convenience of anyone—not even our selfish generation.

The moral nature of our world is a reflection of the holiness of God. God is not subject to external rules. The Ten Commandments reveal rather than control the nature of God. If God were different, the moral structure of our world would be different.

Because of the unique nature of God's holiness, He does not look for opportunities to discard or destroy anyone. When His righteousness has been breached His holiness seeks to redeem. But when His offer of redemption is rejected, the result is justice. Our emotions cry out for a God that will not allow anyone to be lost, even if they choose the way of rebellion. The Bible speaks of a Holy Father, who while giving His best that all may be saved, yet must meet the demands of His own holy nature. He who turned His back on His only begotten Son when Jesus took on himself the sins of the world will never look with pleasure at the unconfessed sins of the human race.

Gratefully, no one need live in a state of panic. The words of the apostle Paul carry great assurance. "Therefore as by the offence of one judgment came upon all men to condemnation; even so by the righteousness of one the free gift came upon all men unto justification of life" (Romans 5:18). John testifies to this grand transaction, "But as many as received him, to them gave he the power to become the sons of God, even to them that believe on his name" (John 1:12). The prospect of hell may be averted, and that eternally, if man will confess his sins and receive Christ as Lord and Savior. But to reject Him is to assure that the final judgment of God upon all sin will certainly fall upon him also.

Which Hell?

Words translated from their original language into the King James Version as "hell," are four in number. The first of these terms is *Sheol* which occurs some 65 times in the Old Testament. Of these, it is translated "grave" 31 times, and in 3 instances "pit" is used. These carry a general meaning of "the place of the dead."

Another term occurring in the New Testament is *Hades.* It too is rather comprehensive, including the realm of the deceased—both the righteous and the unrighteous who await the resurrection. A third term, *Tartaroo,* is used only once in the New Testament and it means to incarcerate (2 Peter 2:4). Because of this broad, ambiguous usage, much misunderstanding has surfaced.

The term with which this chapter is concerned is *Gehenna.* It is defined as the eternal state of the lost after the judgment. Here "hell" properly carries with it all the foreboding so often attached to the name.

It occurs 12 times in the New Testament (Matthew 5:22, 29, 30; 10:28; 18:9; 23:15, 33; Mark 9:43, 45, 47; Luke 12:5; James 3:6). In each instance there can be no mistake about its intended use. Of the 12 occurrences, 11 are in statements attributed to our Lord himself.

Modern translations (note the RSV, NASB, NIV, NEB, as well as the KJV and Wesley, in his *Explanatory Notes upon the New Testament*) consistently use the term *hell* every time where *Gehenna,* the original Greek, is located.

Background of Gehenna

The term comes from the Valley of Hinnon, which has been traditionally identified in the area of the Mount of Olives. It has a morbid history in the Old Testament (1 Kings 11:4-8; 2 Kings 23:10; Jeremiah 7:31; 19:2-6). King Solomon forsook God and turned to idolatry to appease his pagan wives. One of these false gods was Moloch, the god of the Moabites.

Children were burned alive in sacrifice to him. Later it was made a public burning ground for the filth of the city where fires burned constantly. The dead were sometimes cremated there. Criminals were said to have been burned alive at this location. It became an apt emblem of hell itself.

The Synoptic Gospels clearly place the Lord as the Author of this teaching on hell. It may be seen from this written testimony that, for instance, hell was prepared for Satan (Matthew 25:41), and Christ will personally be involved in casting into hell all who do iniquity (Matthew 13:42). This place of eternal judgment is called the "furnace of fire" (Matthew 13:42, 50), and "hell fire" (Matthew 5:22).

Pauline Terminology

Paul did not use the term *hell* when describing the consequences of judgment upon sinful humanity. But he did not leave hope for the rebel heart either. With the second coming of Christ and the Last Judgment, the finally impenitent are banished from the presence of God forever. He uses such phrases as "flaming fire," "everlasting destruction," and "darkness" as the result of God's judgment. The message is clear.

Hell Is Real

Ultimately, what gets to man is the thought that within God's holy love is the provision of hell where the soul may be forever tormented.

Be it torment by material fire which is never quenched, or the eternal anguish of absolute, complete banishment from his Creator, a person would be hard-pressed to describe which is more horrible. John Wesley, in a sermon on hell, uses both metaphors with equal confidence. He says, "Banishment from the presence of the Lord is the very essence of destruction to a spirit that was made for God."[2]

We receive a solemn warning from Mark 9:42-48, that to take the image of hell as symbolic, one must also take the kingdom of God as merely symbolic. To reject the reality of one is to, of necessity, deny the existence of the other.

In hell, the sinner has achieved his own determined goal. He refused the voice of God in life. Now he is forever without it in the living death. He chose to live his whole life to himself. Now he is eternally by himself, though surrounded by the hordes of hell. He wanted nothing to do with God. Now God will have nothing to do with him. Hell may be described as God letting the lost soul do forever what it demanded the right to do while on earth.

Summary

It probably can be said one does not "reconcile" a God of "love" with a doctrine of "hell," if by that one means to draw the two so separated into a neat package, a grand scheme, an eternal ideal.

Hell is a consequent judgment against rebellion in heaven. It was prepared for Satan and his angels. Man was created for God; not hell. After the Fall the Bible reports in Genesis 3 how God builds the bridge back for man. It is made possible through Jesus Christ, His lovely Son.

Christ, however, gives us in the Synoptic Gospels a warning of judgment to come. He uses language which does not imply symbolism. It comprises His strongest warnings to man. To impugn the reality of hell would of necessity cast doubt upon the testimony of Christ and the reality of heaven as well.

This judgment is tied to the final message of God's redemptive plan for man. We have a witness to this in John 3: 16-17. Verse 16 is an often-quoted statement of that self-giving love. But verse 17 says, "For God sent not his Son into the world to condemn the world; but that the world through him might be saved." Saved? Saved from what? Jesus did not come into the world to save sinners from oppression or persecution, but from hell. The story of God's holy love becomes the story of our redemption. But for the finally impenitent there is no other resolution. They have chosen their lot with Satan and will be judged with his judgment—hell.

1. John Wesley, *Explanatory Notes upon the New Testament* (Epworth Press, 1958), p. 122.

2. John Wesley, *The Works of John Wesley* (Beacon Hill Press of Kansas City, Third Edition, 1978), 6:384.

Chapter 7

Question:
Are there any grounds for hope?

God Never Lets Things Just Happen

by Paul Little

Background Scriptures: Genesis 50:20; Daniel 3:17-18; Philippians 1:12-14, 18-20

Have you ever been knocked down by the waves at the seashore? You realize you're in trouble, and you flail around, gasping for breath.

Sometimes life is like that. Tragedy may come; illness may strike; a relationship may fall apart; our financial resources may melt away.

You may not be in such a situation now, but the time will come when the surf of life will knock you down. And then you will want to know how to regain your footing and your spiritual breath.

How can you? The only sure footing in life issues from God. Our confidence in the providential sovereignty of God will anchor our hearts to the fact that our Creator has a loving purpose for each one of us. Nothing happens in your life and mine by accident.

This theme runs through the whole of Scripture from Genesis to Revelation.

Joseph knew it well. He was literally sold down the river by his brothers. In Egypt he was imprisoned because he stood for righteousness. He had every reason for bitterness and hostility, but he was able to say, "You meant it to me for evil, but God meant it to me for good" (Genesis 50:20).

We find the same conviction in Daniel and his three friends, Shadrach, Meshach, and Abednego. King Nebuchadnezzar put it to them clearly: either they must worship his image or be thrown into the fiery furnace. In substance, their answer was, "Look, we don't know what God's plan is, but we believe in his providential sovereignty" (cf. Daniel 3:17-18).

Then there was David whose life hung by a thread for years because King Saul was out to kill him. And David had a lot of friends who wanted to help God out. They said to David, "Look, there's Saul. We'll take care of him for you. The blood won't even be on your hands."

But David, knowing God's providence and love, answered, "The Lord forbid that I should stretch out my hand against the Lord's anointed" (1 Samuel 26:11, NASB).

These and other great men of the Bible knew about the providential sovereignty of God. Of course, they knew Him first as the Lord of their lives, their Deliverer from sin through confession and faith. That relationship is essential.

Let's see how God's sovereignty operated in the life of the apostle Paul. We can see it in the opening chapter of Paul's Letter to the Philippians.

In Philippians 1 Paul is not writing from the local Holiday Inn; he is a Roman prisoner. Yet even in those circumstances he was able to see the providential, loving sovereignty of God operating in his past, his present, and his future.

The whole situation had begun in Jerusalem (Acts 21: 27-40). He had been sent to jail on what we would call a "bum rap" today. He had been wrongly accused of taking a Gentile into the Temple, because the Jews had seen Trophimus the Ephesian with him. In the uproar that resulted he was put into what we call protective custody.

Ultimately, you recall, Paul appealed to Caesar. He was brought to Rome, where he wrote the Philippian Letter. Here he was a prisoner, at first no doubt in a Roman prison. Later he lived in his own lodgings, chained to Roman soldiers on a rotating basis, while awaiting trial under the corrupt, unstable emperor, Nero.

It is in that context that Paul wrote that amazing statement, "Now I want you to know, brethren, that my circumstances have turned out for the greater progress of the gospel" (Philippians 1:12, NASB).

Paul saw the hand of God in his past circumstances. He knew that nothing had happened to him by accident, that God had been working out his purposes. It was this awareness of God's purposeful goodness that kept Paul from being overwhelmed in the surf of life.

Have you recognized that fact about your past? Every one of us has things in his past he wonders about, things he wishes had been different, but it is God who has brought us through. We need to recognize that fact.

God has allowed the struggles which have come into your life, be they relational, financial, or physical. He has allowed stresses. He has been at work in them for your good.

Have you ever thanked Him for His providential, sovereign, and loving care up to the present? Have you been thankful, or have you indulged in second guessing? Maybe you have said, "If only I had said this, or done that, or somebody hadn't done this or that, the whole thing might have been different."

Do you wish you were somebody else or that you were doing something else? You may find yourself fighting God if you fail to realize, as Paul did here, that God has had His hand in all your past.

This may include failures on your part. Though you may have fallen short at certain points, God is most concerned with the present and your relationship to Him from this place on. Whatever may have happened, you didn't take God by surprise. He loves you and He purposes good in all His providential, sovereign working.

However, we need to see that accepting God's providential

sovereignty does not mean we should be passive. It does not mean acceptance of what Muslims call *Kismet,* the blind out-working of fate.

It does not mean that we lack freedom of choice or responsibility. We are to be active where activity is required, but we are to accept that which we cannot control as coming through the hand of God.

When Paul had been falsely accused and thrown in prison in Philippi, he and Silas had sung at midnight. As a result the jailer had been converted and his family with him.

But later, when the magistrates had discovered he was a Roman citizen and wanted him to slip away quietly, Paul had refused. "Nothing doing," he had said in effect. "You violated my rights as a Roman citizen. Come down here personally, get us out of jail and escort us out of town" (Acts 16:37-39).

Paul had accepted the fact that he was in jail, and be-cause of his experience somebody was converted. But later he had made a scene for the glory of God. He had wanted to make it clear to them and to the whole Roman Empire that it was not against the law to preach the gospel.

Paul acted when he could to change the situation; but when he couldn't change things, he accepted them. We should do the same.

Can you recognize the providential sovereignty of God in your present situation? Maybe you are going through something that really troubles you. You do not understand; you don't see how it fits together.

Take courage. Ask God to show you what He is doing. Maybe there are dimensions of blessing that you have over-looked. If you can't see them clearly, realize in the light of the Word of God that He is working in your present circumstances.

Why was Paul used of God even in prison? First, Paul wasn't wallowing in self-pity. He wasn't saying, "Why me?" Paul took his circumstances as from God and made the best of them.

Second, Paul didn't think God had forgotten him. In fact, he took his current situation as an appointment from God. In verse 16 he says, "Knowing that I am appointed for the defense of the gospel."

Do you see what Paul is saying? He is saying, "They know (and they must have gotten it from him) that all these things are part of God's design."

Do you feel God has forgotten you? Remind yourself, as our Lord says in Matthew 10:30, "The very hairs of your head are all numbered." He knows all about that decision or problem or difficulty, and He hasn't made a mistake. He has set you in your situation for a special purpose.

The third reason Paul was used of God was that he lived in the "now." In verse 20 he says it is his hope and earnest expectation that "Christ shall even now, as always, be exalted in my body, whether by life or by death."

Paul could have said, "Well, Lord, I guess this part of my experience is an interlude in my ministry and I can coast." But he didn't. He realized that God's will is not some package in the future, let down from heaven on a string, but a scroll that unrolls each day.

He knew that God had a will and plan and purpose for him today and again tomorrow and the next day. And God has a plan like that for you. The only day you and I have for sure to live for Jesus Christ is now—today.

The Christian life is not some great, successful exploit out in the future. It is an accumulation of days of living for Jesus Christ. Only what you and I put into today will determine the quality and content of our total Christian lives.

Paul also saw the providential sovereignty of God in his future. Circumstances were uncertain; Nero was totally unpredictable. The apostle did not know what the outcome was going to be, but he knew that "this shall turn out for my deliverance" (1:19).

At that point he wasn't talking about being freed from jail, but about his good. Then he says he is in a great tension, desiring that "Christ shall even now, as always, be exalted in my body, whether by life or by death."

Paul wasn't looking to death as a copout, but rather as the

fulfillment of the ministry God had given him. He had confidence in God for the future, whatever it might be.

Your future and mine are uncertain too. But if we have seen the providential sovereignty of God in our past and if we are aware of His presence and power in the immediate present, then we can relax about the way ahead.

Never has there been more uncertainty in the world. There are no entirely safe places, politically, physically, economically. Yet our lives are in God's hands if we belong to Him, and we can trust Him to unfold the future as we are active in working out His purposes.

Nothing happens by accident. And we can rest with confidence in that.

Printed by permission of Marie H. Little, 1980.

Chapter 8

Can You Trust God?

by Elisabeth Elliot Leitch

Background Scriptures: Deuteronomy 6:5-9;
Micah 6:8; Mark 12:28-34

High in the mountains of North Wales in a place called Llanymawddwy lives a shepherd named John Jones with his wife Mari and his black and white dog Mack. I stood one misty summer morning in the window of their farmhouse watching John on horseback herding the sheep with Mack. A few cows were quietly chewing their cud in a nearby corner while perhaps a hundred sheep moved across the dewy meadow toward the pens where they were to be dipped.

Mack, a champion Scottish collie, was in his glory. He came of a long line of working dogs, and he had sheep in his blood. This was what he was made for, this was what he had been trained to do, and it was a marvelous thing to see him circling to the right, circling to the left, barking, crouching, racing alone, herding a stray sheep here, nipping at a stubborn one there, his eyes always glued to the sheep, his ears listening for the tiny metal whistle from his master which I couldn't hear.

Mari took me to the pens to watch what John had to do there. When all the animals had been shut inside the gates, Mack tore around the outside of the pens and took up his position at the dipping trough, frantic with expectation, waiting for the chance to leap into action again. One by one John seized the rams by their curled horns and flung them into the antiseptic. They would struggle to climb out the side, and Mack would snarl and snap at their faces to force them back in. Just as they were about to climb up the ramp at the far end John caught them by the horns with a wooden implement, spun them around, forced them under again, and held them—ears, eyes, and nose submerged for a few seconds.

I've had some experiences in my life which made me feel very sympathetic to those poor rams. I couldn't figure out any reason for the treatment I was getting from the Shepherd that I trusted. And he didn't give me a hint of explanations. As I watched the struggling sheep, I thought, "If there were some way to explain! But such knowledge is too wonderful for them— it is high, they cannot attain unto it." So far as they could see, there was no point whatsoever.

When the rams had been dipped, John rode out again on his horse to herd the ewes which were in a different pasture.

Again I watched with Mari as John and Mack went to work again, the one in charge, the other obedient. Sometimes, tearing at top speed around the flock, Mack would jam on four-wheeled brakes, his eyes blazing but still on the sheep, his body tense and quivering, but obedient to the command to stop. What the shepherd saw, the dog could not see—the weak ewe that lagged behind, the one caught in a bush, the danger that lay ahead for the flock.

"Do the sheep have any idea what's happening?" I asked Mari.

"Not a clue!" she said.

"And how about Mack?" I can't forget Mari's answer:

"The dog doesn't understand the pattern—only obedience."

There are those who would call it nothing more than a conditioned reflex, or at best blind obedience. But in that Welsh pasture in the cool of that summer morning I saw far more than blind obedience. I saw two creatures who were in the fullest sense "in their glory." A man who had given his life to sheep, who loved them and loved his dog, and a dog whose trust in that man was absolute, whose obedience was instant and unconditional, and whose very meat and drink was to do the will of his master. "I delight to do thy will," was what Mack was demonstrating; "Yea, thy law is within my heart."

For Christians, the glory of God's will means absolute trust, it means the will to do His will, and it means joy.

What is this thing called trust? Did Mack's response to John's commands hinge on the dog's approval of the route his master was taking? Mack didn't know what the shepherd was up to, but he knew the shepherd. Have you and I got a Master we can trust? Do we ask first of all to be allowed to examine and approve the scheme?

The apostle Paul admitted the limitations of his own understanding: "Now we know in part," he said, "now we see through a glass darkly." But he was absolutely sure of his Master. He never said, "I know why this is happening," but rather, "I know *whom* I have believed. I am absolutely sure that nothing can separate us from the love of God."

We start, then, with the recognition of who God is. He is

our Creator, the one whose spoken word called into being the unimaginable thing called space which scientists tell us is curved, and the equally unimaginable thing called time which the Bible tells us will cease. He set the stars in their trajectories and put the sliding shutter on the lizard's eye—this is the God who dreamed you up, thought of you before light existed, created you, formed you, and now calls you by name. He says "Fear not, Susan"; He said, "I have redeemed you, Steve."

When the apostle John was an old man in exile on the island of Patmos "on account of the word of God and the testimony of Jesus," he was granted a vision of "one like a Son of man"—eyes like a flame of fire, a voice like a waterfall, His face shining like the full strength of the sun—and in His hand He held seven stars. Old John, who had known and loved Jesus, was overwhelmed. He fell at His feet as one dead. And then the hand that held the seven stars was laid on him, and the voice that was like a thundering cataract said, "Fear not, I *am*—the first and the last; I died, I am alive, I have the keys. Now write what you see."

What John saw turned out to be the Book of the Revelation, the most abstruse of all the books of the Bible, full of bowls of wrath and bizarre beasts, of lightning, and harps, and smoke, and seas of glass, and rainbows of emerald. The courage it took to put all that down in writing for other people to read came from the vision John had had of who it was that was asking him to do it.

It is this same One who asks you and me to do what He wants us to do—the God of creation who's got the whole wide world in His hands. The God who in the person of Jesus Christ "for us men and for our salvation came down from heaven and was made man and was crucified." Those hands that kept a million worlds from spinning into oblivion were nailed motionless to a cross. For us. That hand that held the stars—laid on you. Can you trust Him?

Two thousand years ago Paul said that the Jews were looking for miracles, the Greeks were seeking after wisdom. Not much has changed, has it? People are still looking for instant solutions, chasing after astrologers and gurus and therapists and counselors, but Christianity still has only one story to tell—it's an old, old story: Jesus died for you; trust Him.

Karl Barth was once asked to sum up in a few words all he had written in the field of theology. This was the sum: "Jesus loves me, this I know, for the Bible tells me so."

If you can trust that kind of God, what do you do next? You do what He tells you; you obey. This was the second thing I saw when I watched the shepherd and his dog. If you know your Master, you will to do His will.

This world is His show; He's running it. Do we think of it as under our management? "Do your own thing," they tell us. They even say, "If it feels good, do it." Have you ever heard a more idiotic piece of advice? Is it our world, a sort of make-your-own-sundae proposition, with the will of God just a creamy squirt of earthly success and heavenly approval that goes on top? The will of God is not something you add to your life. It's a course you choose. You either line yourself up with the Son of God and say to the Father, "Thy will be done," or you capitulate to the principle which governs the rest of the world and say, "My will be done."

Harry Blamires has said, "From the human race today goes up one mighty prayer of praise and one tremendous shout of defiance against the loving rule of God. At every moment, and in every act or thought, we swell the volume of that hymn of praise, or else of that cry of blasphemous rebellion."

We identify ourselves with Christ or we deny Him. Jesus chose a path, and went down it like a thunderbolt. When we say as Christ did, "I have set my face like flint to do his will," we are baptized into His death—and like the seed which falls into the ground and dies, we rise to new life. "We have shared his death," Paul wrote to the Romans. "Let us rise and live our new lives with him. Put yourselves into God's hands as weapons of good for his own purposes."

I like that hard, clear language: *put* yourself. Obedience to God is action. I can't find anything about feelings in the Scriptures that refer to obedience. It's an act of the will—"Our wills are ours," wrote Tennyson, "to make them thine." God gave us this precious gift of freedom of the will so that we would have something to give back to Him. *Put* yourself. *Present* your bodies a living sacrifice. Until you offer up your will you do not know Jesus as Lord.

Excerpted from *Questions New Christians Ask*, by Barry Wood. Copyright 1979 by Barry Wood. Published by Fleming H. Revell Company. Used by permission.

Chapter 9

The Glory of God's Will

by Elisabeth Elliot Leitch

Background Scriptures: Psalm 37:3-7;
Proverbs 3:5-6; Isaiah 48:17; Romans 8:28

There are many men and women who have said the eternal
yes to God—"Thy will be done"—but still wonder how they can
know what God wants them to do. They wish that God's orders
were as clear as the pillar of fire to the people of Israel or the
whistle's call to the shepherd dog. How can we possibly know?

Let me tell you a story. When the author of *Christ the Tiger*
was a small boy he used to pull out of the cupboard the paper
bags that his mother saved and spread them around the kitchen
floor. This was permitted on the condition that he collect them
and put them away when he finished playing. One day his
mother (who also happens to be my mother) found the bags all
over the kitchen and Tommy in the living room where his
father was playing the piano. When she called him to pick up
the bags there was a short silence. Then a small voice, "But I

want to sing, 'Jesus Loves Me.'" My father took the opportunity to point out that it's no good singing God's praises while you're being disobedient.

The Epistle of John puts the lesson in much stronger language: "The man who claims to know God but does not obey his laws is not only a liar but lives in self-delusion."

To will to do God's will involves body, mind, and spirit, not spirit alone. Bringing the body under obedience means going to bed at a sensible hour, watching your weight, cutting out the junk food, grooming yourself carefully (for the sake of others). It means when the alarm goes off your feet hit the floor. You have to *move*.

Some of you remember hearing of Gladys Aylward, the remarkable little London parlor maid who went to China as a missionary. She spent seven years there of happy single life before an English couple came to work nearby, and as she watched them she began to realize that she had missed out on something wonderful. So she prayed that God would choose a man for her in England, call him, and send him straight out to her part of China and have him propose. As she told me the story, she leaned toward me, her bony index finger pointing in my face, and said, "Elisabeth, I believe God answers prayer; he called the man—but he never came!" It's a little like the alarm clock: the call to duty comes but *you* have to put your feet on the floor. That's the obedience of the body.

Bringing the mind under obedience for a student means to study. Being in college puts you under a set of obligations. You must pay your tuition, go to classes, write that term paper. You don't need to pray about whether you ought to do these things.

Being a Christian puts you under certain obligations too. You are the salt of the earth, the light of the world, and "my witnesses," Jesus said. You don't need to pray about whether this is God's will or not, but bringing your spirit under obedience entails plenty of praying for understanding and for guidance about the how, when, and where.

The Bible won't tell you whom to marry or what mission field to go to, but I believe with all my heart that as you try honestly to do the things you're sure about, God will show you the things you aren't sure about. We might as well admit that most of our difficulties are not with what we don't understand, but with what we do understand.

In preparation for writing a book on the guidance of God, I read through the whole Bible to find out how He guided people in those days. I found that in the overwhelming majority of cases it was not through what we'd call "supernatural" means —voices, visions, angels, or miracles—but by natural means in the course of everyday circumstances when a man was doing what he was supposed to be doing, taking care of sheep or fighting a battle or mending fishnets.

Just before Abraham Lincoln issued the Emancipation Proclamation, a group of ministers urged him to grant immediate freedom to all slaves.

Lincoln wrote:

> I am approached with the most opposite opinions and advice, and that by religious men who are equally certain that they represent the divine will. I am sure that either the one or the other class is mistaken in that belief, and perhaps, in some respect, both. I hope it will not be irreverent for me to say that, if it is probable that God would reveal His will to others on a point so connected with my duty, it might be supposed that He would reveal it directly to me; or unless I am more deceived in myself than I often am, it is my earnest desire to know the will of Providence in this matter. And if I can learn what it is, I will do it. These are not, however, the days of miracles, and I suppose it will be granted that I am not to expect a direct revelation. I must study the plain physical facts of the case, ascertain what is possible, and learn what appears to be wise and right. The subject is difficult, and good men do not agree.

Lincoln sets for us a sane and humble example. There is no reason to assume that divine guidance is a purely spiritual matter or inward impression. If we belong to the Lord—lock, stock, and barrel; body, mind, and spirit—why should we expect Him to employ only the spirit?

If the question happens to be the matter of becoming a missionary, you have to believe that God has something to do with your even considering such a career. You may seek the advice of godly people whose wisdom you need. You look at a particular need and you may see that you could in fact fill that need. The timing may be right. You have certain gifts—gifts given for the sake of others. Circumstances may point the way. Even your own desires could be sanctified and used for God's purposes—Paul had a streak of romanticism in him, I think, when he said he wanted to preach where Christ had not been named. Why shouldn't God make use of a streak of romanticism? Study the facts. Use your head. Trust the Shepherd to show you the path of righteousness.

One week before I graduated from college, I learned that a young man named Jim Elliot was in love with me. I had been pretty sure for several months that I was in love with him, but kept telling myself that it would be fatuous to imagine that he could ever look twice at me. He was what we used to call a BTO—Big Time Operator, while I was a TWO—a Teeny Weeny Operator. Furthermore he was popular and attractive and I was sure that every little sign that he might be interested in me was only my desperately wishful thinking.

But no, he told me he loved me. My heart turned over and then sank like a stone when he went on to say that he hadn't the least inkling that God wanted him to marry me. He was going to South America, I thought I was going to Africa, and each of us had just been through months of heart searching in an attempt to accept the possibility of life as a single missionary. We believed we had reached that point, and then wham—here we were in love.

How do you discern the will of God when your own feelings shout so loud? We prayed the prayer of Whittier's hymn: "Breathe through the heats of our desire / Thy coolness and Thy balm, / Let sense be dumb, / Let flesh retire, / Speak through the earthquake, wind, and fire, / O still voice of calm."

And one evening as we talked about what was at stake, we agreed that it really was too big for us to handle. God's call to the mission field was strong. Our love was, if anything, stronger. There seemed to be only one thing to do—put the whole thing back into the hands that made us, the hands that were pierced for love of us, and let Him do what He wanted with it. If He didn't want us together, that would be the end of it. If He did, "No good thing will He withhold from them that walk uprightly." We had to believe that promise. Some of you know the end of the story. We waited five years, then God gave us to each other for two years—does this make the will of God even more scary?

But there's a third lesson. The first, remember, as the shepherd and his dog reminded me, was that the glory of God's will for us means absolute trust; the second that it means the will to do His will; and finally it means—believe me—joy. It can't mean anything less from the kind of God we've been talking about.

God made us for glory and for joy. Does He ask us to offer up our wills to Him so that He can destroy them? Does God take the desire of our hearts and grind it to a powder?

Be careful of your answer. Sometimes it seems that God does just that. The rams were flung helplessly into the sheep dip by the shepherd they had trusted. God led the people of Israel to a place called Marah where the water was bitter. Jesus was led into the wilderness to be tempted by the devil. The disciples were led into a storm. John the Baptist, the faithful servant, had his head chopped off at the whim of a silly dancing girl and her evil mother.

Nearly 21 years ago, five American missionaries attempted to take the gospel to a group of jungle Indians who had never heard of Christ. On the eve of their departure they sang together that great hymn by Edith Cherry:

We rest on Thee, our Shield and our Defender,
We go not forth alone against the foe.
Strong in Thy strength, safe in Thy keeping tender,
We rest on Thee and in Thy name we go.

One of the men was Jim Elliot, my husband by that time, who had written in his diary when he was a junior in college, "Father, take my life, yea, my blood if Thou wilt, and consume it with Thine enveloping fire. It is not mine to save; have it Lord, pour it out for an oblation for the world."

Could Jim have imagined how literally that prayer would be answered? Months of preparation went into the effort to reach the Auca Indians of Ecuador. The men prayed, planned, worked, dropped gifts from an airplane, and believed at last that God was clearly showing them that it was time to go. They went, and they were all speared to death.

Five men who had put their trust in a God who represents himself as our Shield and our Defender were speared to death in the course of their obedience. What does that do to your faith?

A faith that disintegrates is a faith that has not rested in God himself. It rests in something less than ultimate, some neat program of how things are supposed to work, some happiness-all-the-time variety of religion. It does not recognize God as sovereign in the world and in the believer's life.

Have you forgotten that we're told to give up all right to ourselves, lose our lives for His sake, present our bodies as a living sacrifice? The word is *sacrifice*. In one of Jim's love letters—and his were different from most, I can assure you—he reminded me that if we were the sheep of His pasture we were headed for the *altar*.

But that isn't the end of the story! To get back to the question as to whether God grinds our hopes to powder, the will of God is *love*. And the love of God is not a sentiment in the divine mind, it's a purpose for the world. It's a sovereign and eternal purpose for every individual life. We follow the One who said, "My yoke is easy," yet His own pathway led straight to the Cross. If we follow Him, sooner or later we must encounter that Cross.

So how can we say that the will of God leads to joy? We can't possibly say it unless we look beyond the Cross—"For the *joy* that was set before him, Jesus endured the cross."

"Everything that happens," says Romans 8:28, "fits into a pattern for good." There is an overall pattern. When my second husband was a boy he always visualized God sitting up there surveying a huge chart. He got this idea from the Lord's Prayer: "Our Father / 'chart in heaven.'"

Last year my daughter and I had tea with Corrie ten Boom. As she talked about her own experience and that of my husband Jim, she took out a piece of embroidery which she held up with the back to us—just a jumble of threads that made no sense at all. She repeated for us this poem which many of you have heard:

> *My life is but a weaving betwixt my God and me,*
> *I do not choose the colors, He worketh steadily.*
> *Ofttimes He weaveth sorrow, and I in foolish pride*
> *Forget He sees the upper and I the underside.*

She then turned the piece over and we saw that it was a gold crown on a purple background.

The shepherd dog doesn't understand the pattern—only obedience. As George McDonald put it, "Obedience is but the other side of the creative will."

The will of God means joy because it is redemptive and it transforms. It is redemptive for it means joy not only for me as an individual but for the rest of the world as well. Did it ever occur to you that by your being obedient to God you are participating with Christ in His death, and then in His redemptive work?

Paul told us this. He said the verse I quoted earlier, "We have shared his death . . . we are weapons of good for his own purposes." Your response helps all the rest of us. Obey God, I say to you, for His sake first of all. Obey Him also for your own sake, for if you lose your life He promised you'd find it. And obey Him, too, for my sake—for the sake of all of us.

There is a spiritual principle here, the same one that went into operation when Jesus went to the Cross. It is the principle of the corn of wheat. The offering up of ourselves, our bodies, our wills, our plans, our deepest heart's desire to God is the laying down of our lives for the life of the world. This is the mystery of sacrifice. There is no calculation where it will end. This is what I mean by transformation.

The bitter water, the wilderness, the storm, the Cross—all are changed to sweetness, peace, and life out of death. God wills to transform loss into gain, all shadow into radiance. I know He wants to give you beauty for ashes. He's given me the oil of joy for mourning, the garment of praise for the spirit of heaviness.

Jim Elliot and his four companions believed that the world and its lust pass away, but He that doeth the will of God abideth forever. Another translation says they are "part of the Permanent and cannot die." In Jim's own words, by giving up what he couldn't keep, he gained what he couldn't lose.

Because of Corrie ten Boom's obedience and that of her family through the hideousness of a concentration camp, because they looked not at what's visible but at what's invisible, hundreds of thousands have seen the light of the knowledge of the glory of God. Jesus had to go down into death; the corn of wheat had to be buried and abide alone in order to bring forth life.

The glory of God's will means trust, it means the will to do His will, and it means joy. Can you lose? Certainly you can lose your life—that's how you find it! "My life," Jesus said, "for the life of the world." What's your life for?

Excerpted from *Questions New Christians Ask*, by Barry Wood. Copyright 1979 by Barry Wood. Published by Fleming H. Revell Company. Used by permission.

Chapter 10

Why Doesn't God Answer My Prayers?

by Barry Wood

Background Scriptures: John 14:5-14; Hebrews 4: 14-15; Romans 8:31-32; Daniel 10:11-13; Matthew 5:23-24; James 4:1-4

Every Christian needs to know more about the miracle and mystery of prayer. This is one area of Christian life in which we never have all the answers. Prayer is a person-to-God encounter and therefore is a profound experience. Prayer, real prayer, is where heaven and earth meet. It is a burning bush: Take off your shoes, you are on holy ground! Because praying is a divine encounter, its mysteries are measureless. God's Word gives us teaching and illustration regarding prayer, but real understanding only comes with experience.

Some of us have had only bad experiences with prayer. In fact, as I write this chapter, it was only last night that I talked to a young adult who said, "I prayed, but it went no higher than the ceiling." We've all felt that emotion! Prayer sometimes is like dialing a phone and getting a busy signal or being put on hold! That's frustrating, to say the least. The young adult I mentioned just had no confidence that God hears and answers prayer. He simply did not know how to "get through" to God.

Why No Answer?

Let me try to give some insight into this crucial need. Everyone needs to talk to our Heavenly Father and needs to know He can and does answer our prayers. So, whenever a believer talks to God and seems to get no answer, why? Why is it that God doesn't always answer our prayers? This is a very real problem, and we need some light from the Scriptures on this matter of unanswered prayer, because he who keeps praying and getting no answer soon quits praying. And he who quits praying loses touch with God and misses life's source of power and blessing.

Unanswered or Unoffered?

James 4:1-4 addresses itself to this problem of unanswered prayer:

> What is the source of quarrels and conflicts among you? Is not the source your pleasures that wage war in your members? You lust and do not have; so you commit murder. And you are envious and cannot obtain; so you fight and quarrel. You do not have because you do not ask. You ask and do not receive, because you ask with wrong motives, so that you may spend it on your pleasures. You adulteresses, do you not know that friendship with the world is hostility toward God? Therefore whoever wishes to be a friend of the world makes himself an enemy of God.

Did you notice that these verses mention several problems affecting our prayer life? Even though unanswered prayer is a problem, there is a greater problem. James says in verse two, ". . . You do not have because you do not ask." Unoffered prayer is our greatest prayer problem. You may wonder why God doesn't respond to you; but, believe me, God wonders why you don't talk to Him more often than you do! You can believe this: God, our Father, wants to answer more requests than we're willing to ask of Him. Jesus said regarding prayer, "Ask and it shall be given to you; seek, and you shall find; knock, and it shall be opened to you. For every one who asks receives . . ." (Matthew 7:7). God wants to answer our prayers. He desires for us to pray. We have not because we ask not.

When Prayer Doesn't Work

Yet, there are times when you do ask, and it may seem, at the time, that prayer doesn't work. When that happens, James, the brother of our Lord, offers us some suggestions why. Whenever our prayers seem not to get through, we need to find what hinders the answers. James suggests we look in three directions.

Look at Yourself. Our prayers are like a missile that is launched into the heavens. A missile is not more successful than the platform from which it is launched. Our lives are the platforms from which prayer is lifted up to the Father. When we pray, God first looks at the "Pray-er," before He listens to the prayer itself. It's the life that prays. Therefore the failure of our prayer to get through may be due to the manner of life we are living. James 4:1-4 describes a life of worldliness. In verse 4, James says, "You adulteresses, do you not know that friendship with the world is hostility toward God?" Our sin can hinder answered prayer. "But your iniquities have made a separation between you and your God, And your sins have hid His face from you, so that He does not hear" (Isaiah 59:2). The Psalmist declared, "If I regard wickedness in my heart, the Lord will not hear" (Psalm 66:18). Notice the phrase, "The Lord will not hear." The Psalmist equated refusal to hear with refusal to answer. God hears all our prayers. Sometimes He just refuses to answer. At other times He just says no and that is His answer.

Therefore, if prayer seems not to work, first examine your heart before God. A pure heart opens the door to God's blessings. First John 3:21-22 says: "Beloved, if our heart does not condemn us, we have confidence before God; and whatever we ask we receive from Him, because we keep His commandments and do the things that are pleasing in His sight." These verses tell us to obey, and our prayers will be answered. God looks at an obedient life before He listens to the prayer. The verb *keep* is in the Greek present tense which indicates a continual habit of life. Thus the Christian who continually lives in obedience can ask whatever he will, and he shall receive, but the believer who only occasionally obeys does not have such a guarantee of answered prayer.

James 5:16 tells us: "The effective prayer of a *righteous* man can accomplish much" (italics added).

As God looks at our lives, He examines our unforgiving spirits. Jesus taught much about prayer and forgiveness. Continually Jesus links the two together. In the Sermon on the Mount He tells us, "If therefore you are presenting your offering at the altar, and there remember that your brother has something against you, leave your offering there before the altar, and go your way; first be reconciled to your brother, and then come and present your offering" (Matthew 5:23-24). He reaffirms this in what we call the Lord's Prayer. "Forgive us our trespasses as we forgive those who trespass against us." Here then is a great principle: You must forgive in order to be forgiven. Bitterness in your heart hinders God from answering prayer.

Sometimes God looks at our **motive in prayer.** "You ask and do not receive, because you ask with wrong motives," says James 4:3. Have you ever prayed for something with a selfish motive? Sure you have. Who hasn't? James says God is not going to answer that kind of praying, so we can go spend it on our pleasures.

I once had a woman ask me to pray for her husband to be saved; then, before I could say I would, she continued, "I've been praying for my husband to be saved, because I can't drive, and every Sunday I have to ride to church with friends and then sit in a couples' Sunday School class. And I'm the only one there without a husband. It's very embarrassing." It doesn't take a wise man to see that her motives weren't too noble!

Wrong motives hinder God's response. Suppose you are

praying for a raise in pay, but you are not honoring God now with the money you have. Why should God give you a raise? To do so would only promote your stealing more from Him! God does look at the manner of our living and the motive of our praying. The only prayer Jesus didn't answer was that of the impenitent thief on the cross. "If You are the Son of God, save Yourself and us," he cried. His motives were impure, and Jesus ignored him. There is a motive that honors God and pleases Him. Jesus said, "And whatever you ask in My name, that will I do, *that the Father may be glorified in the Son*" (John 14:13, italics added).

Look at Your Prayer. If your life and motives are right, what about your prayer? Is it right? Is your prayer in line with God's will? Every prayer prayed according to the will of God gets God's immediate attention.

First John 5:14-15 tells us: "And this is the confidence which we have before Him, that, if we ask anything according to His will, He hears us. And if we know that He hears us in whatever we ask, we know that we have the requests which we have asked from Him." What a glorious truth for those who have lost confidence in prayer! If only we could pray according to God's will, then we could know the answer is on the way. We *have* (present tense) the requests we desired of Him.

Some have observed that faith is what really makes prayer work. They quote Jesus' words, "All things for which you pray and ask, *believe* that you have received them, and they shall be granted you" (Mark 11:24, italics added). Faith is important to experiencing power in prayer, but all the faith in the world will not get an answer to a prayer that is outside the will of God. This is true in regard to miraculous healing. I've seen folks continually believe that God would heal their loved one, then they've watched that precious life die! You see, faith must be founded upon the facts of the Word of God. It is not a fact that God's Word teaches that He wants to heal all sickness. Sometimes what we call faith is nothing more than the power of positive thinking. Faith is more than just believing in our believing. The great issue is not faith, but the sovereign will of God. When my prayer falls in line with God's eternal purposes, then, and only then, can I have boldness before the throne of grace (Hebrews 4:16).

My will or His? That's the question. How can we be sure? No Spirit-filled Christian would deliberately ask for something he knew was not God's will. Yet we often do pray from wrong motives and selfish desires. How can this be corrected? I am convinced there are no foolproof guarantees. Even Paul prayed three times for his thorn in the flesh to be removed, not knowing this wasn't God's will (2 Corinthians 12:7). However, there are some guidelines I've found helpful. First, I must have a yielded life before God—sins confessed up-to-date. Second, I request the Holy Spirit to have full control of thought and deed. Third, I must search the Scriptures for light on the request, to see if it's contrary to biblical truth. Fourth, I pray until He answers or until I get the assurance He's going to answer. Finally He may say no. Then all I can pray is, "Thy will be done."

Look to God. Wait a minute; don't give up yet! There is more here than we've discussed. Who can know the mind of our great God? His thoughts are not ours. In years of learning what prayer is and how to pray effectively, I've learned yet another aspect of prayer not being answered. Often the delay is not due to sin, selfishness, an unforgiving spirit, or the will of God. Sometimes the problem is not with us or our prayer, but rather with God himself. Look at yourself, look at your prayer, then look to God.

A different answer. Sometimes God *is* answering your prayer, but He is answering it differently from the way you desired. This was true of Paul's prayer for God to remove his thorn, as I mentioned. Paul wanted it healed; God wanted to use it to teach Paul valuable lessons of dependence upon His grace. When God answers your requests differently, you just have to trust Him. You know: Father knows best. You may have wanted a *yes* reply and got a *no*. Well, no *is* an answer; isn't it?

A delayed answer. Sometimes God delays the answer, and we mistake the delay for a *no* answer. Our schedule of reply doesn't always match His. You prayed a prayer months ago, and because the answer didn't come when you wanted it to, you thought your Heavenly Father didn't care about you and your needs. He may have been at work all the time! Even while you slept, He was working in answer to your prayer. Even when you had forgotten what you prayed, He was answering.

Do you recall who Zacharias was? He was the father of John the Baptist. Now that's his claim to fame. It took a miraculous answer to prayer to bring that to pass. Zacharias, a priest in the temple at Jerusalem, had no children. His wife, Elizabeth, was barren. Luke records it in his Gospel. "And they had no child, because Elizabeth was barren, and they were both advanced in years" (Luke 1:7). In his old age, as he was going about his Temple duties one day, God sent an angel to him with a message. The message was a strange one. It had to do with a delayed answer to prayer. The angel said, "Do not be afraid, Zacharias, [the angel had a sense of humor because the previous verse describes the terror that came over the old priest at seeing an angel in the Temple!] for your petition has been heard, and your wife Elizabeth will bear you a son, and you will give him the name John" (Luke 1:13).

Old Zacharias was shocked at the message. Why? Because the angel said he had come in response to his prayer! Zacharias had not prayed for a son in years. He had given up on that petition many hugs and kisses ago! He and Elizabeth figured God had said *no* to their youthful prayer. Here is a great principle for us to learn about prayers. God may delay the answer in order to answer it with something better than what we prayed for. Zacharias and his wife requested a son and got a prophet! And what a prophet he was: John the Baptist! You see, often God has more in store for us than we have for ourselves!

Angels and our prayers. There is another reason some answers are delayed. God may have answered your prayer immediately, only to have the answer delayed in transmission. In the previously cited illustration of Zacharias, the priest in the Temple, God sent the mighty angel Gabriel as a messenger to relay His answer to Zacharias. There is another biblical passage which refers to an angel coming in direct answer to prayer. In Daniel 10 we are told that Daniel had been in prayer and fasting for three weeks. At the end of that period, Daniel saw a man in a vision (in reality it was an angel) who had been sent by God in answer to Daniel's prayer. The angel touched Daniel and gave him this strange message: ". . . O Daniel, man of high esteem, understand the words that I am about to tell you and stand upright, for I have now been sent to you . . . Do not be afraid, Daniel, for from the first day that you set your heart on understanding this and humbling yourself before your God, your words were heard, and I have come in response to your words" (Daniel 10:11-12). Before we continue to quote this angel, I want you to note again his words, "from the first day." Daniel had been praying for 21 days and the angel had been traveling 21 days! Now, either heaven is a long way off, or that was some *slow* angel! Not really! There is a third explanation for the delay. Let's read on. "But the prince of the kingdom of Persia was withstanding me for 21 days; then behold, Michael, one of the chief princes, came to help me, for I had been left there with the kings of Persia" (Daniel 10:13).

What are we to make of this statement? The references to princes in verse 13 are references to angels and Satan. The prince of Persia is an allusion to Satan. Michael, the archangel, is a prince of God. Here, then, is a startling conclusion. Daniel prayed a prayer. Twenty-one days passed before an answer came. An angel appeared and told Daniel he had been delayed because Satan hindered him. It took the intervention of a mightier angel, Michael himself, to win the battle. It's as though this angel had been kidnapped, detoured, and defeated, until Michael came to the rescue. All this was going on in the heavenlies while Daniel was praying! If we only knew what spiritual warfares are going on while we pray! So here is another reason some answers are delayed. Satan can hinder and delay the answer.

The Blessing of Unanswered Prayer

Have you ever asked God for something and later been thankful that He didn't answer your prayer? I don't know about you, but I've asked the Father for some rather stupid things that, at the time, I thought were good for me; and it turned out later I was wrong. Praise God for unanswered prayer! We need to believe that our Heavenly Father only wants the best for us; therefore, if an answer is delayed, you can rely upon the fact that He will answer it in a better way. Paul said it well, "What then shall we say to these things? If God is for us, who is against us? He who did not spare His own Son, but delivered Him up for us all, how will He not also with Him freely give us all things?" (Romans 8:31-32).

God does answer prayer. Therefore, when you pray, believe an answer is on the way. It may be *yes;* it may be *no;* or it may be *wait;* but whatever the answer, it will be in your best interest. If it seems God isn't listening, look at your life: Is it free from known sin? Look at your motive: Is it selfish? Look at your prayer: Is it according to God's will? Look to God: Is He delaying the answer or answering it differently?

Then keep praying. "Since then we have a great high priest who has passed through the heavens, Jesus the Son of God, let us hold fast our confession. For we do not have a high priest who cannot sympathize with our weaknesses, but one who has been tempted in all things as we are, yet without sin" (Hebrews 4: 14-15).

Unanswered yet? The prayer your lips have pleaded
  In agony of heart these many years?
Does faith begin to fail, is hope declining,
  And think you all in vain those falling tears?
Say not, the Father hath not heard your prayer,
    You shall have your desire sometime, somewhere.

Unanswered yet! Though when you first presented
  This one petition at the Father's throne
It seemed you could not wait the time of asking,
  So urgent was the heart to make it known;
Though years have passed since then, do not despair,
    The Lord will answer you sometime, somewhere.

Unanswered yet! Nay, do not say ungranted,
  Perhaps your work is not wholly done.
The work began when first your prayer was uttered,
  And God will finish what He has begun.

If you will keep the incense burning there,
His glory you shall see sometime, somewhere.

Unanswered yet? Faith cannot be unanswered
Her feet are firmly planted on the Rock;
Amid the wildest storms she stands undaunted,
Nor quails before the loudest thunder shock,
She knows Omnipotence has heard her prayer,
And cries, "It shall be done, sometime, somewhere."

—Mrs. Ophelia G. Browning

Excerpted from *Questions New Christians Ask*, by Barry Wood. Copyright 1979 by Barry Wood. Published by Fleming H. Revell Company. Used by permission.

Removing the Veil

by A. W. Tozer

Background Scriptures: Romans 5:2;
Ephesians 2:4-8; Hebrews 9:12-14; 10:19

Frederick Faber was one whose soul panted after God as the roe pants after the water brook, and the measure in which God revealed himself to his seeking heart set the good man's whole life afire with a burning adoration rivaling that of the seraphim before the throne. His love for God extended to the three Persons of the Godhead equally, yet he seemed to feel for each One a special kind of love reserved for Him alone. Of God the Father he sings:

> *Only to sit and think of God,*
> *O what a joy it is!*
> *To think the thought, to breathe the name;*
> *Earth has no higher bliss.*
>
> *Father of Jesus, love's reward!*
> *What rapture will it be,*
> *Prostrate before Thy throne to lie,*
> *And gaze and gaze on Thee!*

His love for the Person of Christ was so intense that it threatened to consume him; it burned within him as a sweet and holy madness and flowed from his lips like molten gold. In one of his sermons he says,

> Wherever we turn in the church of God, there is Jesus. He is the beginning, middle, and end of everything to us. . . . There is nothing good, nothing holy, nothing beautiful, nothing joyous which He is not to His servants. No one need be poor, because, if he chooses, he can have Jesus for his own property and possession. No one need be downcast, for Jesus is the joy of heaven, and it is His joy to enter into sorrowful hearts. We can exaggerate about many things; but we can never exaggerate our obligation to Jesus, or the compassionate abundance of the love of Jesus to us. All our lives long we might talk of Jesus, and yet we should never come to an end of the sweet things that might be said of Him. Eternity will not be long enough to learn all He is, or to praise Him for all He has done, but then, that matters not; for we shall be always with Him, and we desire nothing more.

And addressing our Lord directly, he says to Him:

> *I love Thee so, I know not how*
> *My transports to control;*
> *Thy love is like a burning fire*
> *Within my very soul.*

Faber's blazing love extended also to the Holy Spirit. Not only in his theology did he acknowledge His deity and full equality with the Father and the Son, but he celebrated it constantly in his songs and in his prayers. He literally pressed his forehead to the ground in his eager fervid worship of the Third Person of the Godhead. In one of his great hymns to the Holy Spirit, he sums up his burning devotion thus:

> *O Spirit, beautiful and dread!*
> *My heart is fit to break*
> *With love of all Thy tenderness*
> *For us poor sinners' sake.*

I have risked the tedium of quotation that I might show by pointed example what I have set out to say, viz., that God is so vastly wonderful, so utterly and completely delightful that He can, without anything other than himself, meet and overflow the deepest demands of our total nature, mysterious and deep as that nature is. Such worship as Faber knew (and he is but one of a great company which no man can number) can never come from a mere doctrinal knowledge of God. Hearts that are "fit to break" with love for the Godhead are those who have been in the Presence and have looked with opened eye upon the majesty of Deity. Men of the breaking hearts had a quality about them not known to or understood by common men. They habitually spoke with spiritual authority. They had been in the presence of God and they reported what they saw there. They were prophets, not scribes, for the scribe tells us what he has read, and the prophet tells what he has seen.

The distinction is not an imaginary one. Between the scribe who has read and the prophet who has seen there is a difference as wide as the sea. We are today overrun with orthodox scribes, but the prophets, where are they? The hard voice of the scribe sounds over evangelicalism, but the Church waits for the tender voice of the saint who has penetrated the veil and has gazed with inward eye upon the Wonder that is God. And yet, thus to penetrate, to push in sensitive living experience into the holy Presence, is a privilege open to every child of God.

With the veil removed by the rending of Jesus' flesh, with nothing on God's side to prevent us from entering, why do we tarry without? Why do we consent to abide all our days just outside the holy of holies and never enter at all to look upon God? We hear the Bridegroom say, "Let me see thy countenance, let me hear thy voice, for sweet is thy voice and thy countenance is comely." We sense that the call is for us, but still we fail to draw near, and the years pass and we grow old and tired in the outer courts of the tabernacle. What doth hinder us?

The answer usually given, simply that we are "cold," will not explain all the facts. There is something more serious than coldness of heart, something that may be back of that coldness and be the cause of its existence. What is it? What but the presence of *a veil in our hearts?* A veil not taken away as the first veil was, but which remains there still shutting out the light and hiding the face of God from us. It is the veil of our fleshly fallen nature living on, unjudged within us, uncrucified and unrepudiated. It is the close-woven veil of the self-life which we have never truly acknowledged, of which we have been secretly ashamed, and which for these reasons we have never brought to the judgment of the Cross. It is not too mysterious, this opaque veil, nor is it hard to identify. We have but to look in our own hearts and we shall see it there, sewn and patched and repaired it may be, but there nevertheless, an enemy to our lives and an effective block to our spiritual progress.

This veil is not a beautiful thing and it is not a thing about which we commonly care to talk, but I am addressing the thirsting souls who are determined to follow God, and I know they will not turn back because the way leads temporarily through the blackened hills. The urge of God within them will assure their continuing the pursuit. They will face the facts however unpleasant and endure the cross for the joy set before them. So I am bold to name the threads out of which this inner veil is woven.

It is woven of the fine threads of the self-life, the hyphenated sins of the human spirit. They are not something we do, they are something we are, and therein lies both their subtlety and their power.

To be specific, the self-sins are these: self-righteousness, self-pity, self-confidence, self-sufficiency, self-admiration, self-love, and a host of others like them. They dwell too deep within us and are too much a part of our natures to come to our attention till the light of God is focused upon them. The grosser manifestations of these sins—egotism, exhibitionism, self-promotion—are strangely tolerated in Christian leaders even in circles of impeccable orthodoxy. They are so much in evidence as actually, for many people, to become identified with the gospel. I trust it is not a cynical observation to say that they appear these days to be a requisite for popularity in some sections of the Church visible. Promoting self under the guise of promoting Christ is currently so common as to excite little notice.

One should suppose that proper instruction in the doctrines of man's depravity and the necessity for justification through the righteousness of Christ alone would deliver us from the power of the self-sins; but it does not work out that way. Self can live unrebuked at the very altar. It can watch the bleeding Victim die and not be in the least affected by what it sees. It can fight for the faith of the Reformers and preach eloquently the creed of salvation by grace, and gain strength by its efforts. To tell the truth, it seems actually to feed upon orthodoxy and is more at home in a Bible conference than in a tavern. Our very state of longing after God may afford it an excellent condition under which to thrive and grow.

Self is the opaque veil that hides the face of God from us. It can be removed only in spiritual experience, never by mere instruction. As well try to instruct leprosy out of our system. There must be a work of God in destruction before we are free. We must invite the Cross to do its deadly work within us. We must bring our self-sins to the Cross for judgment. We must prepare ourselves for an ordeal of suffering in some measure like that through which our Savior passed when He suffered under Pontius Pilate.

Let us remember: when we talk of the rending of the veil we are speaking in a figure, and the thought of it is poetical, almost pleasant; but in actuality there is nothing pleasant about it. In human experience that veil is made of living spiritual tissue; it is composed of the sentient, quivering stuff of which our whole beings consist, and to touch it is to touch us where we feel pain. To tear it away is to injure us, to hurt us and make us bleed. To say otherwise is to make the Cross no cross and death no death at all. It is never fun to die. To rip through the dear and tender stuff of which life is made can never be anything but deeply painful. Yet that is what the Cross did to Jesus and it is what the Cross would do to every man to set him free.

Let us beware of tinkering with our inner life in hopes of rending the veil ourselves. God must do everything for us. Our part is to yield and trust. We must confess, forsake, repudiate the self-life, and then reckon it crucified. But we must be careful to distinguish lazy "acceptance" from the real work of God. We must insist upon the work being done. We dare not rest content with a neat doctrine of self-crucifixion. That is to imitate Saul and spare the best of the sheep and the oxen.

Insist that the work be done in very truth and it will be done. The Cross is rough, and it is deadly, but it is effective. It does not keep its victim hanging there forever. There comes a moment when its work is finished and the suffering victim dies. After that is resurrection glory and power, and the pain is forgotten for joy that the veil is taken away and we have entered in actual spiritual experience the presence of the living God.

Lord, how excellent are Thy ways, and how devious and dark are the ways of man. Show us how to die, that we may rise again to newness of life. Rend the veil of our self-life from the top down as Thou didst rend the veil of the Temple. We would draw near in full assurance of faith. We would dwell with Thee in daily experience here on this earth so that we may be accustomed to the glory when we enter Thy heaven to dwell with Thee there. In Jesus' name, Amen.

Taken from *The Pursuit of God,* by A. W. Tozer, and used by permission of Christian Publications, Inc., Harrisburg, PA 17101.

Chapter 12

Question:
Is there a spirit world?

Angels, Demons, and the Devil

by Ivan A. Beals

Background Scriptures: Job 38:4-7; Psalm 103:19-20; Hebrews 1:6-14; Revelation 12:7-12

People respond to life in various ways, and for different reasons. Many follow the bumper-sticker slogan, "If it feels good—do it!" Ads convince them, "You only go around once in life, so grab all the gusto you can." Pleasure is eagerly sought to enjoy life for the moment—little else matters.

Yet, mankind is haunted by horrifying experiences and visions of doomsday. Popular movies depict natural disasters, nuclear holocaust, the exorcism of demons, the plight of zombies, interplanetary visitors, and wars. A nagging thought persists that life is not simply confined to the material realm.

Men in every place and time have pondered their relation to God, to nature, and to the universe. A recent Gallup Poll found more than half of all adult Americans have had a lasting "born-again" Christian experience. But another poll says 40 percent of American teenagers believe in astrology. Increased interest in the cults, from transcendental meditation to witchcraft, from spiritualism to fortune-telling, illustrates man's search for a sure answer to life's meaning.

The Bible reveals two levels of life where reality is encountered. There, the Divine and the human meet, the spiritual and the material realms intersect, and the unity of life is seen above the conflict of good and evil. A religious dualism is disclosed—a division between the natural and the supernatural, the seen and the unseen.

The Scriptures view man as a spirit-soul-body unit (1 Thessalonians 5:23), so living occurs in multidimensions. A person discerns self-awareness, with moral choices, in the physical realm and the mysteries beyond it. Some call the spirit world the "other" world, in contrast to this material world.

Our concern about the spirit world regards angels, the devil, and demons, and what happens when a person dies. Though Christians may also be anxious about the future, superstition and fear are more apt to plague those who face the unknown without faith in God and salvation through Jesus Christ. A biblical understanding of the spirit world begins with faith in a supreme Creator, who assures personal life with purpose and destiny.

This discussion will broach several issues:

★ Are angels actual creatures or phantoms?
★ Why are angels used in some situations and not others?
★ Does sensitivity to God's will contribute to one realizing the presence of angels?
★ Why, since the Scripture teaches about supernatural beings, do we think of them differently than people did in Bible times?
★ How are angels involved with believers at death?
★ If the devil and demons exist, did God create evil?

Angels

As the firstborn over creation, Jesus Christ is declared the Creator of all things: "things in heaven and on earth, visible and invisible" (Colossians 1:16, NIV).* Paul further states, "He is before all things, and in him all things hold together" (v. 17).

The Bible reveals two classes of intelligent creation—angels and men. "Angels" denotes an office, not a nature. The Greek word *angelos* means a messenger, or one sent on an embassy. Angels are spiritual beings, superior to man, dwelling in the heavenly regions. They were fashioned in the image and likeness of God, as was man (cf. Genesis 1:26; 2:7)—"a living being."

Scriptures put these spiritual intelligences first in rank and point of time among created beings. The Lord declares "the morning stars sang together and all the angels shouted for joy," when the cornerstone of the earth's foundation was laid (Job 38:7; cf. Psalms 103:19-20; 148:1-2). David states man was made "a little lower than the heavenly beings" (Psalm 8:5; cf. Hebrews 2:5, 7). So, angels are more powerful than bold men (2 Peter 2:11; cf. 2 Thessalonians 1:17).

Angels are numerous. Ten thousand angels confirmed the presence of God on Mount Sinai as He gave the Law of Moses (Deuteronomy 33:2). "The chariots of God are tens of thousands and thousands of thousands" (Psalm 68:17; cf. Matthew 26:53). Speaking of the heavenly Jerusalem, "the city of the living God," Hebrews 12:22 declares, "You have come to thousands upon thousands of angels in joyful assembly."

The Bible mentions different ranks or offices among angelic beings. Michael, whose name means "Who is like unto the Lord?" is called the archangel (Jude 9). The prefix "arch" suggests a chief position. The Lord tells Daniel that Michael is "the great prince who protects your people" (Daniel 12:1; cf. 10:13, 21). His position and office join those of the Messiah (cf. Revelation 12:7-11). "For the Lord himself will come down from heaven, . . . with the voice of the archangel

*Unless otherwise noted, all scripture quotes in this chapter are from *The Holy Bible, New International Version.*

and with the trumpet call of God, and the dead in Christ will rise first" (1 Thessalonians 4:16).

The angel named Gabriel, meaning "God is mighty," is mentioned four times in the Bible, always the bearer of good news. He announces the vision for the "end time," revealing God's plan in history (Daniel 8:15-16; cf. 9:21 f.). Gabriel also foretells the birth of John the Baptist (Luke 1:19), and he informs Mary she is to be the mother of Jesus, "the Son of God" (Luke 1:26 f.).

The cherubim and seraphim differ in rank from the archangel and angels. Peter may refer to these angelic "authorities and powers in submission to him" (1 Peter 3:22). Though they are real and powerful, their mention in Scripture is often symbolic of heavenly things.

God employs angels in behalf of the righteous on earth. A mounted host was sent to protect the prophet Elisha from the Syrian army (2 Kings 6:14-17). "The angel of the Lord encamps around those who fear him, and he delivers them" (Psalm 34:7). To King Darius, Daniel declares, "My God sent his angel, and he shut the mouths of the lions" (Daniel 6:22). Peter was released from prison by an angel of the Lord (Acts 12:7). An angel of God also comforted Paul before the shipwreck on his way to Rome (Acts 27:23). "Are not all angels ministering spirits sent to serve those who will inherit salvation?" (Hebrews 1:14).

Angels are used of God to issue judgment against the wicked. "He unleashed against them his hot anger, his wrath, indignation and a hostility—a band of destroying angels" (Psalm 78:48; cf. Isaiah 37:36). At the judgment, the "Ancient of Days" is attended by thousands upon thousands of angels (Daniel 7:9-10). In the last days, seven angels will pour the wrath of God out of seven golden bowls (Revelation 15—18).

Jesus taught that angels would come and separate the wicked from the righteous in the last day (Matthew 13:39-49). "For the Son of Man is going to come in his Father's glory with his angels, and then he will reward each person according to what he has done" (Matthew 16:27). He will send His angels with a loud trumpet call, "and they will gather his elect" (24:31; cf. 2 Thessalonians 1:7).

Angels are not to be worshiped. Paul warns, "Do not let anyone who delights in . . . the worship of angels disqualify you for the prize" (Colossians 2:18). When John the Revelator fell down to worship a heavenly messenger, the angel said, "Do not do it! I am a fellow servant with you and your brothers who hold to the testimony of Jesus. Worship God" (Revelation 19:10; cf. 22:9).

Like man, all angels were created morally accountable to God. For some period, they were in a testing-state when they could resist God's rule (cf. Psalm 103:19-20; Matthew 6:10). Jude tells of "the angels who did not keep their positions of authority but abandoned their own home—these he [the Lord] has kept in darkness, bound with everlasting chains for judgment on the great Day" (v. 6).

The Devil and Demons

Even the evil angels were once holy and happy, but they chose against that exalted state. Jesus taught of Satan's fall, saying, "He was a murderer from the beginning, not holding to the truth" (John 8:44; cf. Luke 10:18). Christ's judgment of the wicked will be: "Depart from me, you who are cursed, into the eternal fire prepared for the devil and his angels" (Matthew 25:41). Peter declares, "God did not spare angels when they sinned, but sent them to hell, putting them in gloomy dungeons to be held for judgment" (2 Peter 2:4).

John says there was war in heaven. Michael and his holy angels fought against the evil dragon and his angels. "The great dragon was hurled down—that ancient serpent called the devil or Satan, who leads the whole world astray. He was hurled to the earth, and his angels with him" (Revelation 12:9; cf. 12:7-12; Matthew 12:24).

There is a real, personal devil revealed to us in various ways. Both Adam and Christ, who had no bent toward sin, were tempted (cf. Genesis 3; Matthew 4); Adam fell, but Christ was sinless. Among the many miracles Jesus performed, He cast out seven demons from Mary Magdalene (Luke 8:2) and delivered a man, called Legion, from many demons (8:27-31).

Some people's acts, attitudes, and passions are ascribed to the devil and to demons. Satan entered Judas Iscariot when he went out to betray Jesus (Luke 22:3). Peter warns, "Your enemy the devil prowls around like a roaring lion looking for someone to devour" (1 Peter 5:8). John declares, "He who does what is sinful is of the devil . . ." (1 John 3:8).

We must put on the whole armor of God to survive the devil's schemes. "For our struggle is not against flesh and blood, but against the rulers, against the authorities, against the powers of this dark world and against the spiritual forces of evil in the heavenly realms" (Ephesians 6:12; cf. 6:11-17).

God allowed Satan to afflict Job (1:6-12), and no doubt demons inflict some of man's present diseases. They also influence the minds and hearts of men to evil. Paul notes the "ruler of the kingdom of the air, the spirit who is now at work in those who are disobedient" (Ephesians 2:2). Speaking of the man of sin, the antichrist, Paul declares, "The coming of the lawless one will be in accordance with the work of Satan displayed in all kinds of counterfeit miracles, signs and wonders, and in every sort of evil that deceives those who are perishing" (2 Thessalonians 2:9-10a).

While Christians are aware of the occurrence of demon possession in our day, these should not be confused with mental illness. Be aware that "the cravings of sinful men, the lust of his eyes and his pride in possessions" (1 John 2:16) give occasion for Satan and his cohorts to rule a person's life. On the other hand, Christians may suffer mental illness caused by severe emotional stress and shock, or by serious physical disease. Many people profit from prescribed medicines and professional care, as well as the healing wrought by prayers of faith.

The devil and his demons thus corrupt our world, and perhaps other parts of the universe. Evil spirits are so many that a legion, 6,000, were in possession of one man. Their number explains the tempter's apparent omnipresence. Though they try to destroy the lives of men, they can only tempt and influence to evil. But they cannot coerce us to sin. If we "resist the devil," he will flee from us (James 4:7).

A Personal Angel Ministry

A father and daughter were driving out of Lincoln, Neb. As the father drove into an intersection with the right of way, a glistening white angel seemed to appear on the hood of the car. The angel's wings spread over the windshield, blocking the view. The father jammed on the breaks. Just then, from the left, another car sped by in front of them, barely missing a smashup. Both father and daughter said they saw the angel, that he faced the direction from which the other car came. Without the angel's warning, serious injury or death would have occurred.

David says, "He who dwells in the shelter of the Most High will rest in the shadow of the Almighty. . . . For he will command his angels concerning you to guard you in all your ways" (Psalm 91:1, 11). Perhaps every believer has a guardian angel, from infancy. Jesus said, ". . . do not look down on one of these little ones. For I tell you that their angels in heaven always see the face of my Father in heaven" (Matthew 18:10).

Jesus said angels rejoice over one sinner who repents (Luke 15:10). We are "in the sight of God and Christ Jesus and the elect angels" (1 Timothy 5:21). Paul says God has made each Christian "a spectacle to the universe, to angels as well as to men" (1 Corinthians 4:9). Whether we realize it or not, our personal lives are in the presence of angels.

Because an "angel of the Lord" acted in Jesus' resurrection (Matthew 28:2-4), we may expect angels to assist us in death. Jesus told of a beggar named Lazarus, who died and was carried by angels to paradise (Luke 16:19-24). "Precious in the sight of the Lord is the death of the saints" (Psalm 116:15). David declared, "Yea, though I walk through the valley of the shadow of death, I will fear no evil" (Psalm 23:4, KJV).

Our triumph can't be blasted by the devil or his demons, but neither do we overcome by the strength of angels. Final victory is by the blood of the Lamb and the word of our testimony (Revelation 2:11). Thus, in our lives Romans 8:38 becomes reality: "For I am convinced that neither death nor life, neither angels nor demons, neither the present nor the future, nor any powers, neither height nor depth, nor anything else in all creation, will be able to separate us from the love of God that is in Christ Jesus our Lord."

Chapter 13

> *Question:*
> **Is there life after death?**

God and Death

by Levitt/Weldon

Background Scriptures: Job 19:21-27; 17:24;
1 Corinthians 15:51-53; 2 Corinthians 5:8;
Philippians 1:21-23

According to the Bible everyone will experience life after death. The question is not whether an individual will enter eternity, but *where* he will spend it.

The Bible discusses death practically. It shows the way to prepare for it and it tells about the life that follows.

Comparing for a moment the biblical life after death with the occult views of life after death we find them utterly opposed. The Bible, as we will show, indicates that the dead may not be contacted and that no one living may go into the "next world" to check out death (or at least it must always be a one-way trip). Those who died formerly in unbelief are confined, as we will see, and those who died believing we shall encounter only later on. Consulting mediums to attempt communication with the dead is expressly prohibited in the Bible:

> Do not turn to mediums or spiritists; do not seek them out to be defiled by them. I am the Lord your God *(Leviticus 19:31, NASB)*.

> Should not a people consult their God? Should they [instead] consult the dead on behalf of the living? *(Isaiah 8:19, NASB)*.

But people have always been fascinated with the possiblity of consulting the dead despite God's admonitions. So zealous an Israelite as King Saul consulted a medium with drastic results (see 1 Samuel 28): "So Saul died for his trespass which he committed against the Lord, because of the word of the Lord which he did not keep, and also because he asked counsel of a medium, making inquiry of it, and did not inquire of the Lord. Therefore He killed him" (1 Chronicles 10:13-14, NASB).

Apparently contact with the dead is God's province exclusively. We feel that the contactees of the mediums are demonic because, according to the Scriptures, they cannot be the actual dead. We also feel that the biblical admonition against such exercises ought to be taken seriously.

Instead, the Bible says we are to take the Word of God at face value and count on the sacrifice of Christ to take us into eternal life. Any inquiry we may have on behalf of the dead can be answered through prophecy and the biblical passages which account for the disposition of all souls who ever lived.

The Resurrection and the Life

The near-death experience of a Christian believer which we will now present greatly differs from the reports given earlier in the secular research. At this point we need to reemphasize that, believer or nonbeliever, these experiences are the exception, not the rule.

Betty Malz had been in a coma for 44 days, hovering between life and death. At the time she had the following experience. The resuscitation instruments had already been disconnected and a sheet pulled over her face. She was assumed dead. Her father knelt by her bedside in prayer.

But the patient was aware of her father's prayer; "All he could say was 'Jesus, Jesus!'" she reports. Her story continues:

As he was saying this, I was approaching a beautiful hill. To the right of me was a silvery marble wall. At the top of the hill were gates of pearl. I heard resounding voices of worship, an angelic chorus singing, "Glory to the name of Jesus." I joined the singing.

The angel to the left of me asked, "Would you like to go in and join the chorus?"

"No," I answered. "I would like to sing for a while, and then I'd like to go back to my family."

He nodded. I turned around and went back down the hill, and as I went the sun was rising over the beautiful marble wall.

In my room the early morning sun rays were pouring through the clear window over the air conditioner near my bed. Often, I have seen dust particles dancing in sun rays. But as I looked at these rays slanting across my bed, I could see ivory letters about two inches high go before my vision like a stock market tape report. And these were the words: St. John 11:25—"I am the resurrection and the life: he that believeth in me, though he were dead, yet shall he live."

I reached out in wonder to take hold of these words of God. In doing so, I pushed back the sheet covering me and touched those words with my hand. When I did this, life came into my fingers, through my arms and all through my body—and I pushed back the sheet and sat up. No man can take credit for my healing, the Word of God healed me.

My father was simply overwhelmed. Although he had seen God heal people in answer to prayer during his ministry, he had never seen anything like this!

The nurse's aide who had been attending me and was in the room at the time went into immediate action. She ran out of the room screaming, "It's a ghost!"

And no one could get her to come back in during the 48 hours following that I was still in the hospital.

Doctors, nurses, newspapermen, a Catholic priest, and some sisters began coming into my room to ask me all about it. It was a joy for me to share with them what had happened and to give testimony for my Lord.

That remarkable experience served to enhance the faith of the subject considerably. Very much alive today, she says,

"Now I know the joy of living and testifying for Jesus and praising His name. Now I truly appreciate the privilege of knowing Christ personally and serving Him."

So the first difference between the above testimony and the life-after-life experiences reported in the secular research is the difference in the reaction by the subject. Mrs. Malz now continues in her faith, her walk with the Lord enhanced, and her doctrine and beliefs in no way changed. This is a far cry from the reassuring but questionable, "Now I know we have nothing to worry about. Everyone is accepted after death." The latter of course contradicts the Bible, not to mention the moral reckoning of any number of nonbiblical civilizations. As we said earlier it seems to represent an example of demonic activity meant to lead men astray.

Mrs. Malz's experience had no hint of judgment—not even a "review" of her life followed by the rubber-stamp acceptance. There is no judgment in the case of a believer since Christ was already punished on the believer's behalf (Romans 8:1).

There were no earthly characters in Mrs. Malz's experience —no "living dead" to assist her passage. There was no Being of Light, but the Lord's presence was indicated by the song of praise. The experience contained highly relevant scriptural commentary for Mrs. Malz to understand and profit by, and obviously she has.

Now of course, we would be advocating a double standard if we said that Mrs. Malz died and came back to life and the secular folks were only fooled by demons. In fact, we must continue with our contention that no one who is alive was ever dead, including Mrs. Malz. It is the *kind or quality* of experience we wish to emphasize in this case. Unbelievers seem to experience false doctrine of a kind specifically attributed to Satan in the Bible; believers (and there are other similar cases) experience doctrinally accurate events, which might come right out of the Scriptures. We *would* expect the presence of angels, songs of praise, and lessons in scripture in the hereafter, to take the Bible at face value. All of these are replete throughout the Book of Revelation in its heavenly scenes. And we *would* expect the utter absence of all of those things, or some crude masquerades, in the case of unbelievers. That is, biblically, the way things are.

Where Are the Dead?

A lot of people have died. Where are they?

The Bible speaks to that very plainly. And it divides all past mankind into two large groups—the saved and the un-saved. Salvation, as we said, refers explicitly to death; from death we are saved, to go to eternal life. Some say we are saved from sin but they mean the same thing ("The wages of sin is death"). Sin means separation from God and those who die in sin, unsaved, will be away from the presence of God forever, according to the Scriptures. Those whose sins are forgiven, via the payment made by Jesus Christ, are reconciled to God and thus defeat death.

The Bible comments at length about the position of the *saved* dead. They go to be with the Lord:

> For to me to live is Christ and to die is gain . . . having a desire to depart and to be with Christ, which is far better *(Philippians 1:21, 23).*

The apostle considers departing to be with Christ as "far better" than remaining alive. Death is "gain" to Paul, since he anticipates the very presence of the Lord.

In Luke 23:43 (NASB), the Lord himself clearly indicates that the saved dead join Him. He tells the repentant thief on the cross:

> Truly I say to you, today you shall be with Me in paradise.

On other occasions this overwhelming promise issued from the lips of the Lord. In His reassuring Upper Room discourse He told the disciples about His going to prepare a place for them so that "where I am, there you may be also" (see John 14: 1-3, NASB). Speaking in the context of eternal life He repeated "where I am, there shall My servant also be" (John 12:26, NASB). And He prayed:

Father, I desire that they also, whom Thou hast given Me, be with Me where I am, that they may behold My glory [My final triumph] *(John 17:24, NASB)*.

Paul wrote to the Church at Corinth in terms of his yearning "to be absent from the body and to be at home with the Lord" (2 Corinthians 5:8, NASB).

Even those future believers, slain after the Rapture of the Church in the coming period of Great Tribulation (see Matthew 24), are seen in prophecy as being with the Lord and speaking to Him (Revelation 6:10 ff.).

The martyr Stephen (Acts 7) accused his tormentors of heresy, proved his point from the Scriptures and was stoned to death in perfect faith. He had not the vaguest doubt that the Lord would be ready to receive him immediately upon his death and he preached the same with his dying breath, "Lord Jesus receive my spirit" (vv. 55-59).

This, then, is the joy of the believer. If the Scriptures are to be taken seriously, there *is* abundant life after death and it awaits the follower of Christ. The saved dead are undoubtedly with Him in heaven. They will dwell eternally in the presence of God.

Not so, however, with the *unsaved dead,* God's second large category of men. The Bible's most unpopular passages deal with the confinement and punishment of those who died, and *will* die, in unbelief. "No decent God would punish human beings," say the humanitarians and religionists who wish to escape the uncomfortable biblical future for unbelievers. "I don't want any God who cannot see how worthy I am." The litany of rebelliousness, begun in the Garden goes on and on.

But the Scriptures are very clear. The Lord sounded enough warnings for the entire human race to hear ("You fool, this very night your soul is required of you!"—Luke 12:20, NASB). Jesus told His disciples that they need not fear killers among men, "who kill the body, and after that have no more that they can do." Those killers only cause the first death, the physical death. They are fearful enough, of course, but the Lord's point was to warn of the wrath of a righteous God, who has sway over the final death: "Fear the One who after He has killed has authority *to cast into hell;* yes, I tell you, *fear Him!"* (Luke 12: 4-5, NASB).

Curiously, some people who swear by the passages on heaven in the Bible utterly reject the passages on hell, and obviously this is not rational. The vast majority of our clinical death reports were replete with quasi-heavenly scenes, but missing were the signs of the other side of things. No judgments, no troubles, nothing but pure acceptance awaits us all, according to those reports. But it seems obvious that the "heavenly" parts of those scenarios were drawn from the scriptural ideal. What represented all the scriptures which frankly report on hell? If the Bible contains both, how did those reports get so selective?

Apparently we experience what we *want* to experience, and we censor out what might make us unhappy. We can actually kid ourselves to hell, as it were.

Hell is described in the Bible in a variety of terms: "outer darkness," "the resurrection of judgment," "the place where there is weeping and gnashing of teeth," "eternal punishment," etc. But why would it have to be described as eternal? Probably because no amount of punishment *in time* has any *meaning* when compared to the *eternity* of eternity, and because without the punishment of evil, there is no justice. In eternity, there *is* no time, hence, if in eternity there is to be any justice—any punishment of evil—it must last forever, or else be ultimately meaningless. The problem is not that hell exists—it must exist if God is infinitely holy and any distinction is to be made between good and evil. A Hitler or Stalin must not go unpunished. The problem is that men do not understand how *evil* sin *is* when compared to a Being who is *truly,* infinitely holy—that the smallest sin is justly worthy of eternal punishment. Since God is infinitely just, the eternal punishment of sin can be no more or less severe—or just—than that which is demanded by the case. If hell is real, and it is, remember also:

God is not wishing for any to perish, but for all to come to repentance. He desires all men to be saved and to come to the knowledge of the truth *(2 Peter 3:9; 1 Timothy 2:4, NASB).*

and,

For God so loved the world that he gave his only begotten Son that whosoever believeth in him should not perish but have everlasting life *(John 3:16).*

If the Son of God himself had to die a horribly torturous death, and had to have the judgment of all men's sins *placed on Him* simply to allow for the possibility of man's salvation, we must not think God will go lightly with those who act as if He doesn't even care.

A number of verses in the Bible refer to a specific place of confinement for the unsaved dead. Jesus spoke of a hypocrite whose faith in his master was not real: "The Master of that slave will come on a day when he does not expect him . . . and assign him a *place* with the unbelievers" (Luke 12:46-47, NASB). The rich man wanted to warn his brothers lest they come "to this place of torment" (Luke 16:28, NASB). The betrayer Judas "went to his own place" (Acts 1:25, NASB).

The Epistles of Peter are conclusive in this regard. Through 1 and 2 Peter the apostle refers to the disobedient spirits "now in prison" (1 Peter 3:19; 4:6, NASB) and the shining angels being committed by God to "pits of darkness reserved for judgment." Peter concludes:

The Lord knows how to rescue the godly from temptation, and to keep the unrighteous *under punishment* for the day of judgment *(2 Peter 2:9, NASB, italics added).*

Without wishing to sound like "hellfire and damnation" preachers, we must still elucidate these verses so relevant to our discussion. It's a highly metaphysical or spiritual point, but if the *unsaved dead* are confined and the *saved dead* are with Christ, then no one has seen any dead person, except perhaps in rare circumstances where God permits it with believers as in the case of Samuel.

We could discuss at length the impossibility of valid

communication with the unsaved dead in the biblical view. They are simply not reachable. That situation would upset God's doctrine on life and death entirely. This is not to say, of course, that demon activity could not result in a deception; if we are subject to occultic experience, we may experience just about anything the devil can dream up to divert us. But it does go to say that the Bible knows of no going and coming between life and death. If in Luke 16 the unsaved dead could not even cross over to the realm of the saved, it seems clear they cannot "come over" to the living.

Dr. Merrill Unger's definitive *Bible Dictionary* sums up:

> The blessed dead being with Abraham were conscious and "comforted" (Luke 16:25). The dying thief was on that very day to be with Christ in "Paradise." The unsaved were separated from the saved by a "great gulf fixed" (Luke 16:26). The rich man, who is evidently still in Hades, is a representative case and describes the un-judged condition in the intermediate state of the wicked. As to his spirit, he was alive, fully conscious and in exercise of his mental faculties and also tormented. It is thus apparent that insofar as the unsaved dead are concerned, no change in their abode or state is revealed in connection with the ascension of Christ. At the sinners' judgment of the Great White Throne, Hades will surrender the wicked. They will be judged and be cast into the Lake of Fire (Revelation 20:13-14). That the human spirit continues to exist consciously after the death of the body is a fact most clearly established upon a biblical basis; to say nothing of the strength of philosophical arguments upon the matter. That a most powerful contrast is declared between the state of the righteous and that of the wicked not only after the final judgment, but also during the interval between that event and the death of the body should also be regarded as beyond question.

Thus there are but two kinds of men, whether one considers past, present, or future. Those who believe in God and His plan of salvation through the vicarious sacrifice of Jesus Christ have one expectation, and those who don't have the other. The people who died before us are accounted in one of the two groups and those who come after us fall under the same economy. And finally, all of those alive now may choose, as all men have chosen, their group. The way of salvation is, of course, always open to all men.

The people already dead are out of our reach completely. The Bible speaks of no "visitation" possibility. The Bible cannot conceivably be reconciled to any life-after-death experience reported by a living individual. Life after death, in the biblical view, is possible for any person, but it is obtained through the principles of the gospel of Christ and never by any human preparation, acts of merit, or scientific phenomena.

God awards eternal life on the basis of faith.

Hell on Earth

Hell is not really so hard to imagine. We just have to look at what's going on among us now.

"How can there be a hell?" is one of the unbiblical person's constant questions. Nobody likes the idea of hell, least not of all God, who has gone to some real trouble to preserve and sanctify His children. But we have some very real intimations of hell on the earth right now, in our daily papers.

Hell must be a place where the most evil thoughts of a vast community of men gain free reign. Hell must be a place where all the Hitlers and Stalins who have ever lived compete for power (for not just those demigods, but all of us who would, given the chance, act as they did!). Hell must be where there is no further alternative—where the war is never over, the frustration never eased, the prayer always hopeless.

Theologians—serious Bible scholars—have wrestled with the matter of hell for ages. The true Bible believer is not proud or conceited in his gift of salvation (Ephesians 2:8-9) but rather very humbled. It is obvious at least up to this point in history that a majority of men will not qualify under God's plan of salvation as matters stand, and that's troubling. The Lord commanded us to "love all men," and believers cannot be satisfied with the worldly situation.

This is an awful world, presently. No matter what is said about our plight today by optimistic scientists, false religionists, or the occultists who see better things ahead after death, this is an awful world. And this awful world bodes nothing but more awfulness for the future.

People are starving and no one feeds them. People are oppressed and other people sell them out for political gain. The military forces in the world may blow the whole place up at any time and we all know it. Most thinking people would not be at all surprised by the arrival of a nuclear war that will reduce this planet and all it contains to poisoned rubble. The Armageddon of the Bible, that final holocaust, seems too near, too much on our present agenda.

How can God sit through all this? Why doesn't He do something?

Well, of course, He *has* done something. Who would do more than "lay down His life for His friends"?

We know of no other authority than the Bible in the discussion of life after death. We have given the various views as we find them today. But we find them wanting compared to the timeless, relevant message of the Word of God. We have accurately and patiently tried to trace man's latest ideas about his most engaging and troubling question—where he's really going when he dies. But we have more or less come home again—back to the Bible.

We just don't trust those reports and we've given our reasons. We certainly would never gamble with the message of salvation and how it is obtained in God's will. We would not take a chance on hell for anything. We would not take the new courses in how to pass smoothly over into death for fear of offending the Creator of life, and we think that stands to reason.

At this point we should like to summarize and pull together our discussion. What are our conclusions to date?

In certain cases where reasonable evidence exists, the out-of-the-body experiences may be real. For example, when a revived patient, who was unconscious, describes the doctors actions in accurate detail. It is also at least possible that the experience, or most of them, could be totally in the brain. However, the realm of reality and unreality is by no means easily distinguished once demonic influences enter the picture. A demonic capacity clearly exists to manipulate a person's mental state to such a degree that the unreal illusion becomes experienced as totally real.

If the experiences are real, however, it is crucial to recognize they do *not* represent the totality of what really happens at death. The use of real experiences which validate a false world view has always been a key tactic of the enemy. In the clinical death phenomena—although the experience, or at least parts of it, may be real enough—the interpretation placed upon it (e.g., there is nothing to fear in death) is false.

A simple half-minute out-of-the-body experience in and of itself would not necessarily remove the fear of death with the degree of conviction as represented in the clinical death cases. However, it is another story when they occur in *near death states,* and when *dead friends and relatives* are seen in perfect health and contentment, and when a "being of light" emanating great love and joy appears with a comforting message. These additional elements of the experience cause the conviction that death is a "friend," a friend who represents the transition to greater happiness, instead of an enemy who brings eternal judgment.

Whether or not an OBE, assuming it is real, is of God or Satan depends on whether the experience itself, and its impact, is biblical or not. Obviously, religious but nonbiblical messages from a "being of light" or "the dead" are not of God. This isn't to say that Christians, in rare circumstances may not have OBEs in the near-death state. When we die, the spirit does leave the body (Ecclesiastes 12:7; Luke 8:55; 1 Kings 17:21-23). God is sovereign and can do as He pleases. God may reveal part of the spirit realm if it suits His purposes, as He did with Paul and Elisha (2 Corinthians 12; 2 Kings 6:17. These experiences were, however, of a different nature than the clinical death ones). Paul also states he didn't *know* if he was in the body or not, i.e., he couldn't tell—and that he was not permitted to speak about what he did see. This experience is in contrast to those of today. The Christian is to "walk by faith, not by sight."

Eternal life with God is magnificent! The prospect is the

111

happiest thought the human mind can think. Just writing about what's going to happen to those who've chosen God is a wonderfully rejuvenating endeavor.

What's more precious than life?

Eternal life!

Quoted from *Is There Life After Death?* by Levitt/Weldon. Copyright 1977 by Levitt/Weldon. Used by permission of Harvest House Publishers, 2861 McGaw, Irvine, California 92714.